QUILTS FOR MANTELS & MORE

11 Delightful Designs

SUSAN THOMSON

Martingale™
& COMPANY

Credits

President . . . . Nancy J. Martin
CEO . . . . Daniel J. Martin
Publisher . . . . Jane Hamada
Editorial Director . . . . Mary V. Green
Managing Editor . . . . .Tina Cook
Technical Editor . . . . Erana Bumbardatore
Copy Editor . . . . Allison A. Merrill
Design Director . . . . Stan Green
Illustrator . . . . Robin Strobel
Cover Designer . . . . Stan Green
Text Designer . . . . Regina Girard
Photographer . . . . Brent Kane

That Patchwork Place® is an imprint
of Martingale & Company™.

Quilts for Mantels and More:
11 Delightful Designs
© 2002 by Susan Thomson

Martingale & Company
20205 144th Avenue NE
Woodinville, WA 98072-8478 USA
www.martingale-pub.com

Printed in China
07 06 05 04 03   8 7 6 5 4 3 2

Dedication

To my husband, John, the most patient man in the world. I cannot imagine my life without his love, his support, and his unending talent for computer design.

Acknowledgments

My special thanks go to my wonderfully supportive family, without whom I could not possibly have had the courage to write this book.

To Terri Burton and the staff and teachers at Quilt 'n Sew Studio in Katy, Texas, for their help and support, and for allowing me to teach my patterns.

To the quilters at Quilt 'n Sew—Fran Stromberg, Diane Labunsky, and Barb Knoblock—who gave me their time when time was short and always shared their ideas and talent.

To my best friends, Suzanne Cordova and Clydene Hellenguard, and my mom, Sue Rawley, for their help sewing the samples.

And finally to my students, who were often guinea pigs for my designs in the works.

Library of Congress Cataloging-in-Publication Data

Thomson, Susan.
    Quilts for mantels and more : 11 delightful designs / Susan Thomson.
        p. cm.
    ISBN 1-56477-430-9
    1. Machine quilting—Patterns. 2. Patchwork—Patterns. 3. Mantels. I. Title.
TT835 .T4637 2002
746.46' 041—dc21   2002007632

Mission Statement

We are dedicated to providing quality products and service by working together to inspire creativity and to enrich the lives we touch.

Contents

Introduction

If you're reading this book, it's a given that you love quilts and quilting—just like me. But no matter how much we enjoy quilting, there's a limit to how many bed quilts any one of us can actually make in one lifetime. I will make as many as my fingers and time will allow, but sometimes it's great to start a project that's a little smaller, a little simpler, and that I know I can

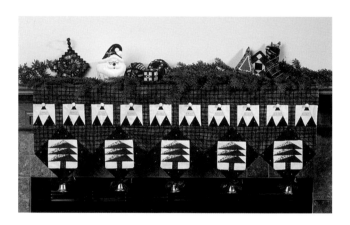

finish. In keeping with my love of all things quilted and the warmth of that patchwork feeling, I've designed a series of quilts especially for your fireplace mantel. The blocks are almost entirely paper pieced, so they're quick to make and sure to draw the admiration of quilters and nonquilters alike. Plus, these great designs adapt beautifully to use as window valances, table runners, and smaller door quilts, letting you extend the look that we all love to virtually every room in your house.

All the projects in this book include step-by-step cutting and stitching instructions, as well as tips and patterns that let you adapt the designs to other uses in your home, making them as easy to construct as they are to decorate with. You can follow my directions exactly or use them as a jumping-off point, choosing just the right fabrics and colors to complement your decor perfectly. I hope my quilts can add warmth and beauty to your home throughout the seasons.

Susan Thomson

Getting Started

Tools and Supplies

Paper piecing requires very few items that any quilter wouldn't already have on hand.

Sewing machine. The most important tool you'll need to paper piece successfully is a sewing machine in top working order that can do a straight stitch. Set it to fifteen to eighteen stitches per inch. If your machine has "needle up/needle down" capability, set it to "needle up."

Machine needles. For paper piecing on a sewing machine, you'll find that a size 90/14 needle is helpful because it creates larger holes. This will make your job much easier when it's time to remove the paper.

Thread. Good-quality, all-cotton thread in a medium gray shade is perfect for use in scrappy projects because it blends well with both light and dark fabrics.

Scissors. You'll need a pair of high-quality, sharp shears for use on fabric only, and a pair of medium-quality scissors sharp enough to cut through fabric and paper. Embroidery scissors or thread snips are great for "unsewing" when you need to remove a seam; I find they work a little better than a seam ripper.

Rotary-cutting supplies. As with any quilting project, you'll need a rotary cutter, a mat, and an acrylic ruler. My favorite ruler size for these projects is 6" x 12", but you may also find a 6" x 24" ruler handy for cutting longer pieces.

Fabric adhesive. A roll-on temporary adhesive, found at office-supply stores, is great for temporarily holding fabric pieces in place before stitching.

Pressing tools. A wooden "iron" is handy for pressing seams while paper piecing. Many people feel this saves their fingers from becoming sore when they're doing a lot of piecing at once.

Turning tool. This tool is useful for poking out turned corners and points. A large crochet hook or a wooden spoon handle also works well.

tip Use two rotary cutters, labeling one "fabric only" and the other "paper only." This will help keep your fabric blade from dulling too quickly.

Selecting Fabrics

All-cotton fabric rules the quilting world, and I recommend using the best-quality quilting fabric you can afford. The designs in this book require mostly small- to medium-scale prints in rich tones. I almost always choose prints that have lots of rich colors and very little light background. Shirting fabrics—the kind that were once used to make men's shirts and pajamas—are my favorites as backgrounds; they're white or light-colored, with small, geometric prints in navy, red, or brown. I often use more than one background fabric, to add richness and texture. Small checks, plaids, and homespuns contribute greatly to the warm feel of the designs in this book. Overall, I've chosen fabrics with

a relaxed look that's homey, comfortable, and easy to incorporate into an existing decor.

Choosing backing fabric for mantel quilts is easy for me: I always use unbleached muslin. The simple reason for using this plain, homey, and inexpensive fabric is that the back of a mantel quilt will never show unless you choose to turn it over and show it!

The back of your window valance, on the other hand, may be visible through the window, so select a backing fabric you'd like to be seen from the outside. If you have blinds, sheers, or other window coverings behind the valance and therefore the backing won't show, muslin is still a good, inexpensive choice. Even if your backing will show, an advantage of muslin or another light-colored fabric is that exposure to sun won't fade it—a definite concern if lots of unfiltered light will be coming through the window. If you want to prevent your piecing seams from showing through your valance, choose a thicker backing, such as drapery-lining fabric.

Batting

I like to use very low-loft batting in projects like those in this book. A flat, old-fashioned look is best for these country-home designs. Plus, you don't want extra loft puffing up a mantel quilt that will likely have items placed on top of it. Flannel and Pellon Fleece are also good choices for the middle layer of a mantel quilt.

Whether you should use batting in a window valance depends on the look you're trying to achieve. Valances with batting look more substantial, giving a cornice effect; valances without batting look lighter. Batting in valances also provides some insulation—although this is not something I need, living in south Texas! Refer to the individual projects for more on batting use.

tip If you're in a hurry to finish your valance and you don't have any drapery-lining fabric handy, use a layer of batting. It will solve the show-through problem just as well.

Adapting the Projects

The projects in this book have both elements with fixed sizes (the paper-pieced blocks) and elements that you will customize to fit your particular mantel or window (the top-of-mantel fabrics, casings, backings, and battings). Directions for determining how many blocks you'll need and the size to cut customized pieces are at the beginning of each project, but each mantel quilt or valance starts with the same step: measuring.

Mantel Quilts

To begin, measure your mantel along its length. Round this measurement down to the nearest whole inch; then add ½" and write the number down. This is the length of the top-of-mantel fabric you need. This number also governs how many blocks you'll make. (Each project will tell you how to calculate the number of blocks needed.)

Next, measure the depth of your mantel, from the wall to the outside edge. Round this measurement down to the nearest whole inch; then add ½" and write the number down. This is the width of the top-of-mantel fabric you need.

Window Valances

Before you measure for your window valance, decide on the look you want and the type of curtain rod you will use. If you want the valance to hang *inside* the window frame on a tension rod, measure the distance between the two inside edges of the window frame. If you want the valance to hang *outside* the window frame on a regular rod, measure the distance between the two places where the rod will be attached to the wall. (Similarly, if you want the valance to hang on the front rod of a double rod, measure the distance between the two places where the front rod is attached to the back rod.) The resulting measurement is the width of your valance.

Paper Piecing

If you're new to paper piecing, you're in for a treat. Paper piecing allows you to make fast, accurate, identical blocks that have seam intersections you'd never be able to piece the traditional way. It's easy to learn, and it lets you take your quilting to a whole new creative level.

The Basics

To make any of the projects in this book, first make copies of the patterns you'll need for the paper-pieced blocks. You'll need one copy for each block required for your quilt. (See individual projects to determine how many blocks you'll need.) You may need to make more than one copy of a particular unit to complete a single block. The easiest way to copy the patterns is on a photocopy machine. Make a test copy first, comparing it to the original for size and quality. Always copy from an original pattern; never copy another copy. Use paper made for this purpose, such as Papers for Foundation Piecing from That

Patchwork Place, or use copy paper. If you choose to use copy paper, use 20# or lighter (my favorite is 18#, but it's hard to find). The advantage to lighter-weight paper is that it's easier to remove, but don't go any lighter than 18# or use tracing or tissue paper; they can tear away before you're ready.

After copying the patterns, trim around them, leaving ¼" to ½" of paper outside the dotted cutting lines. (Later, you'll trim both paper and fabric.) The right side of the pattern, which is the side you'll sew on, is marked with lines and numbers. The wrong side, which is the side you'll position your fabric on, is unmarked.

tip   Keep in mind that if the block you're making is asymmetrical, the printed side of your pattern will be the mirror image of your finished block.

Once your patterns are copied and trimmed, set your sewing machine to fifteen to eighteen stitches per inch and insert a new size 90/14 needle. Now you're ready to paper piece.

1. Referring to the cutting chart for your block (see individual projects), cut a piece of fabric for area 1. Position it right side up on the unmarked side of the pattern, making sure it is large enough to cover area 1 plus at least ¼" on all sides. Hold the pattern and the fabric up to the light to make sure you have covered area 1, then use roll-on adhesive or a pin to hold the fabric in position.

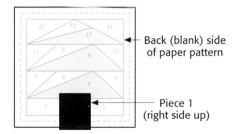

Back (blank) side of paper pattern

Piece 1 (right side up)

2. Refer to the cutting chart to cut a piece of fabric for area 2. Position it right side up on the unmarked side of the pattern over the area marked 2, making sure it covers all of area 2 plus ¼" on all sides. Then flip piece 2 so that the right sides of pieces 1 and 2 are together, making sure

piece 2 extends at least ¼" into area 2. Fix piece 2 in place with roll-on adhesive or a pin.

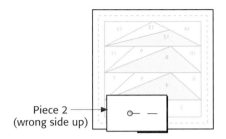

Piece 2 (wrong side up)

3. Turn the pattern over to the marked side, and sew directly on the seam line between areas 1 and 2, extending your seam line ¼" beyond the ends of the line. (The seam will be crossed by other seams, so there's no need to backstitch.)

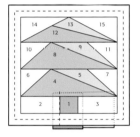

4. Cut the threads close to the paper on the front and back. Trim the seam allowance, leaving a scant ¼".

5. Fold back piece 2 to cover the area marked 2. Finger press or use a wooden pressing tool. Hold the pattern up to the light to check for proper positioning.

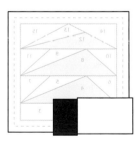

6. Refer to the cutting chart to cut the piece for area 3. Working on the seam line between areas 2 and 3, repeat steps 2–5. Continue adding pieces in numerical order until the pattern is complete.

7. Press the fabric side of the completed pattern with a hot iron.

8. If the finished block has multiple units, piece each of the units individually. Then trim the units carefully on the dashed lines, place them right sides together, and stitch on the solid lines to join the units together.

9. Even if the pattern is one where the paper will not be removed (see page 9), remove the paper from the seam allowances of multiunit patterns so the seams between them will lie flat when pressed open.

Power Paper Piecing

Take the speed and accuracy of paper piecing to a whole new level by chain-piecing units just as you would in traditional patchwork. With this method, you'll finish the multiple blocks most designs require in a fraction of the time and with a minimum of effort. I recommend that you complete one of each kind of block you'll need before you begin chain piecing. This way you'll be able to get a feel for the pattern and color placement before cutting fabric for all the blocks in your quilt.

1. After you've finished your test blocks, refer to the project's cutting chart to cut the required number of pieces for each unit in all of your blocks. Keep the pieces separated and labeled by number and unit so you'll be able to locate the piece you need quickly.

2. Position a piece 1 and a piece 2 on the wrong side of a pattern, pinning or using temporary adhesive to hold the fabrics in place, if desired. Check the positions of the pieces, flip the pattern over, and stitch the seam between the pieces. Immediately position another piece 1 and piece 2 on the next pattern (using a pin or temporary spray adhesive to hold them in place), butt it up against the first pattern, and stitch the seam between those pieces. Don't stop between patterns to cut the threads—just let them stack up behind your machine as you keep feeding patterns through. If the stack gets too tall, clip the thread and start another stack.

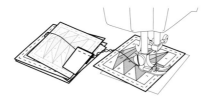

tip   Once you're comfortable with power paper piecing, try it without pinning your pieces in place for an even faster finish!

3. When all the pieces 1 and 2 are sewn to the patterns, clip the threads between the blocks, trim the seam allowances to ¼", and press the seams.

4. Add piece 3 to all your patterns in the same manner.

5. Continue until all the patterns are completed. The last time you clip, trim, and press, all your blocks will be finished—at the same time.

Once I started using this method, I could never go back to starting and completing a single block and then starting over on the next block. Try it—you'll be hooked!

One word of caution: This can be a wonderfully mindless activity, but if you're thinking about your next project and not about the pattern at hand, you can make a mistake on many blocks, not just one!

Trim Carefully

As simplistic as it sounds, the careful trimming of the completed patterns on the dashed lines is extremely important to the accuracy of the finished quilt. If you have trimmed carefully, when you join two patterns by stitching along the solid line of one pattern, you will also be stitching through the solid line on the other pattern. All of your points will match perfectly, every time.

tip   If you discover that you've forgotten to trim a seam allowance before proceeding to the next numbered area, don't worry. After the paper is removed, you can trim any seam allowances you missed.

Paper Removal

When making a mantel quilt or valance, you can remove the paper patterns from the blocks after you've sewn them into rows. However, if you won't need to wash the mantel quilt or valance, you have the option of leaving the paper patterns attached to the bottom row of blocks. This gives the on-point row some weight, which helps it hang nice and straight.

When making a regular-size quilt or table runner, remove the paper patterns after the rows have been joined together.

When the time comes to remove paper from the edges of a pattern, tear into the paper to the seam and then tear along the seam. This will prevent popped

stitches at the ends of seams. A slight pull will release the paper from the stitching line.

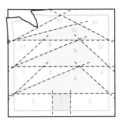 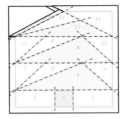

tip Paper removal is a great job for kids—unfortunately, you may find that you have to pay them to do it!

Assembling and Finishing

Once the blocks are made, it's time to put the projects together. Each project has directions for assembling individual rows, but all the mantel quilts are constructed with the same basic elements and techniques.

Adding Setting Triangles

All of the mantel quilts and some of the other designs in this book contain blocks set on point. In the mantel quilts, on-point blocks form the bottom that hangs over the edge of the mantel. These on-point blocks are joined together with setting triangles. There will always be one fewer setting triangle than blocks, and there will always be two end triangles.

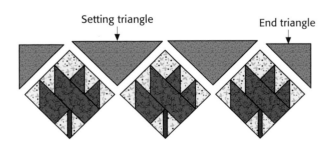

1. Refer to your project's directions to determine the number and size of squares to cut to make setting triangles. Cut the squares in half diagonally in each direction to make 4 quarter-square triangles.

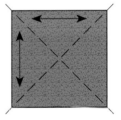 

Quarter-Square
Setting Triangles

2. Refer to your project's directions again to determine what size to cut a square to make the end triangles. Cut the square in half once diagonally to make 2 half-square triangles.

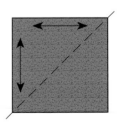 

Half-Square
Corner Triangles

3. Align the edge of a block with a short edge of a setting triangle, making sure the right angle of the triangle lines up with the right angle of the block, as shown. Sew the block and triangle together and press. There will be excess fabric at the top of the row because all the setting triangles in this book are cut oversize. The excess fabric will be trimmed away later.

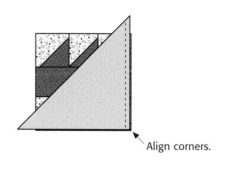

Align corners.

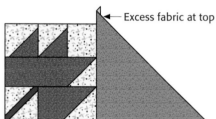

Excess fabric at top

4. Sew a block to the other short edge of the setting triangle, aligning the upper left edge of the second block with the other short triangle edge. Make sure the second block extends ¼" past the seam you just sewed. Stitch the seam with a standard ¼" seam allowance, turn the block over, and press.

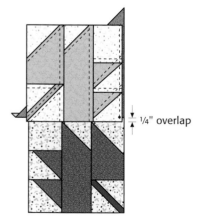

¼" overlap

5. Repeat steps 3 and 4 to add blocks and setting triangles to complete the row.

6. Finish the row by sewing the long edge of an end triangle to each end of the row. Once again, align the triangles so that any excess fabric falls at the top of the row, where it will be trimmed off later.

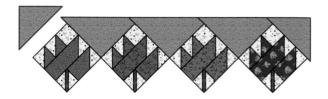

7. Carefully clip ⅛" into the seam allowance at the inner point where the block joins the setting triangle. This helps the seam allowance to lie flat.

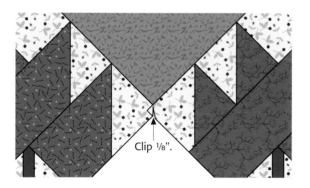

Clip ⅛".

8. Use your rotary cutter and ruler to trim away excess fabric from the top edge of the row, ¼" above where the blocks join the setting triangles. (This is the seam allowance between this row and the one above it.) Move the ruler along the entire length of the row, measuring and trimming. (Depending on the length of the row, a 24" ruler might make this step easier.)

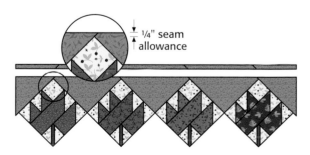

¼" seam allowance

Layering and Finishing

All of the mantel and valance quilts in this book have an envelope finish. The "Autumn Color Table Runner," "Winter Chill Wall Quilt," and "Baby's First Little Quilt" have straight-grain bindings.

Envelope Finish

1. Place the rectangle of batting on the bottom and the rectangle of backing on top of it, right side facing up. Lay the mantel quilt top, right side facing down, on top of the backing rectangle. You should have at least 2 inches of extra batting and backing all the way around the quilt top.

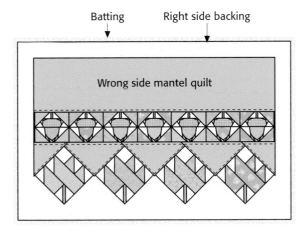

Batting   Right side backing

Wrong side mantel quilt

2. Baste the layers together with quilter's safety pins, starting in the center and working out to the edges. Place pins no further than 6" apart, and don't close the pins until they are all in.

3. Use a ¼" seam allowance to stitch around the quilt top and through all the layers, pivoting sharply at the points. Leave a 6" opening along the top edge for turning.

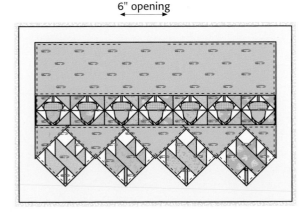

6" opening

4. Trim, trim, trim—this is an important step. Trim away the excess backing and batting, leaving a ¼" seam allowance around the quilt top. Trim an additional ⅛" of batting from the seam allowances to keep it from "squishing" out and blunting the points of your blocks.

5. Carefully clip ⅛" into the seam allowances at the inside points between the blocks and the setting triangles. This will give you nice, sharp inner points.

6. Turn the project right side out through the opening and poke out the points with a turning tool or the end of a wooden spoon or large crochet hook. Work gently, being careful not to poke through your quilt, but do try to get very sharp points at the block tips and corners. Press with a hot iron until your mantel quilt lies smooth and flat.

7. Turn under the raw edges of the opening and hand stitch it closed.

Straight-Grain Binding

See the individual project directions to determine how much binding to cut. Once you've cut your strips, follow these directions to bind your quilt.

1. Trim the backing and batting even with the quilt top.

2. With right sides together, join the binding strips at right angles, stitching across the corners and trimming seam allowances to a scant ¼" as you go. Press the seams open.

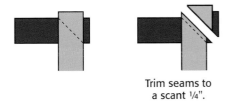

Trim seams to a scant ¼".

3. Cut one end at a 45° angle, and fold it under ¼". Fold the binding strip in half along its length, wrong sides together, and press.

4. Beginning in the center of one side, place the angled end of the binding strip on the quilt top, raw edges even with the edge of the quilt top. Starting a few inches from the end of the binding strip, attach the binding with a ¼" seam allowance, stopping and backstitching ¼" from the corner of the quilt.

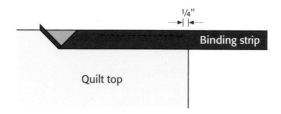

5. Clip the thread and turn the quilt so you can stitch down the next side. Fold the binding up and away from the quilt, keeping the raw edge in line with the right edge of the quilt.

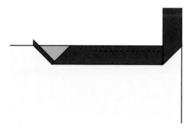

6. Fold the binding back down onto itself, keeping the raw edges aligned, and begin stitching ¼" from the corner, backstitching to secure.

7. Repeat steps 5 and 6 to finish attaching the binding. When you get back to the start of the binding strip, overlap it by about 1", cut away the excess, trim the end at a 45° angle, and tuck the end into the beginning. Finish sewing the seam.

8. Fold the binding to the back of the quilt. Blindstitch the binding in place by hand, covering the machine stitching as you go. Blindstitch the corner miters in place as you stitch.

Quilting

The type and amount of quilting you do is up to you. All of the projects in this book are machine quilted in the ditch between the major seams, and some have additional decorative stitching. Refer to the individual projects for ideas on quilting and embellishing.

Christmas Santa Mantel Quilt

Finished block sizes:
Tree on point—5⅝" x 5⅝"; 8" across diagonal
Santa—3" x 3"

Materials

Yardages are based on 42"-wide fabric.

- ¾ yd. dark green print for Tree blocks, setting rectangles, and setting triangles*
- ½ yd. light print for Tree and Santa block backgrounds
- ½ yd. red print for Santa blocks and triangles around Tree blocks
- ¼ yd. light green print for Tree blocks
- Scraps of dark brown for tree trunks
- Scraps of flesh tone for Santa faces
- Scraps of white for Santa beards
- Tiny pompons, jingle bells, or tassels for embellishments

* The quilt shown uses 2 different dark green prints, but you could use ¾ yd. of the same fabric throughout the quilt.

NOTE: Yardages are based on the quilt shown. If your quilt requires more blocks than shown, you may need to buy extra fabric.

Measuring Your Mantel

Refer to "Adapting the Projects" on page 6 to measure the length and width of your mantel. You will need the following additional materials based on these measurements.

Top-of-mantel fabric: 1 piece the size determined *70 ½ x 10 ½*
Backing fabric: 1 piece 2" longer and 2" wider than top-of-mantel fabric *72 ½ x 12 ½*
Batting: 1 piece the same size as backing fabric *72 ½ x 12 ½*

Determining the Number of Blocks

Tree blocks: Divide the length of your mantel in inches by 8. Round down to the next whole number for the number of Tree blocks to make.

Santa blocks: Divide the length of your mantel in inches by 4. Round down to the next whole number for the number of Santa blocks to make.

Cutting for One Tree Block

Cut 1 piece of fabric for each piece number, unless otherwise indicated.

Piece	Fabric	Dimensions
1	Dark brown	1½" x 1½"
2, 3	Light print	1½" x 2½"
4, 8	Dark green print	2" x 5"
5, 9	Light green print	1½" x 4"
6, 7, 10, 11	Light print	2¼" x 2¼" ⧅ *
12	Dark green print	1¾" x 5"
13	Light green print	1½" x 3¾"
14, 15	Light print	2¼" x 3"

⧅ Cut in half diagonally once to yield 2 triangles.
* *Cut 2 squares for these pieces.*

Cutting for One Santa Block

Cut 1 piece of fabric for each piece number.

Piece	Fabric	Dimensions
1	White	2½" x 2½"
2, 3	Red print	2½" x 2¼"
4	Flesh tone	2½" x 1½"
5	White	1¼" x 2"
6	Red print	1¾" x 1¾"
7, 8	Light print	2¼" x 4¼"

Additional Cutting

From the dark green print, cut:

1 square, 10" x 10", for every 5 Tree blocks your mantel requires; cut each square diagonally twice to yield 4 setting triangles. (You may have leftover triangles, depending on the number your quilt requires.)

1 square, 5¼" x 5¼"; cut diagonally once to yield 2 end triangles

1 strip, 1½" x 42"; subcut into 1½" x 3½" rectangles to yield 1 fewer rectangle than you have Santa blocks

From the red print, cut:

2 squares, 4" x 4", for each Tree block; cut each square diagonally once to yield 4 triangles for each Tree block

Making the Blocks

Referring to "Paper Piecing" on page 6 and using the cutting charts at left and the patterns on page 45, make the number of Tree blocks and Santa blocks your mantel size requires.

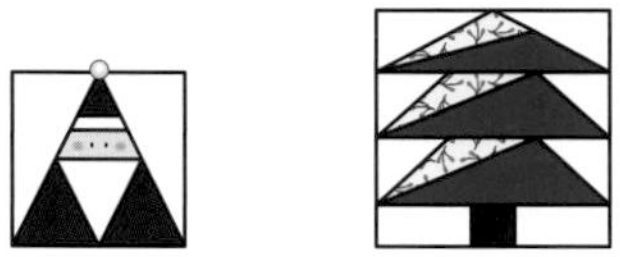

Santa Tree

Assembling the Tree Row

1. Sew 2 red print triangles to opposite sides of a Tree block. Press toward the triangles. Sew 2 more red print triangles to the remaining sides. Press toward the triangles again.

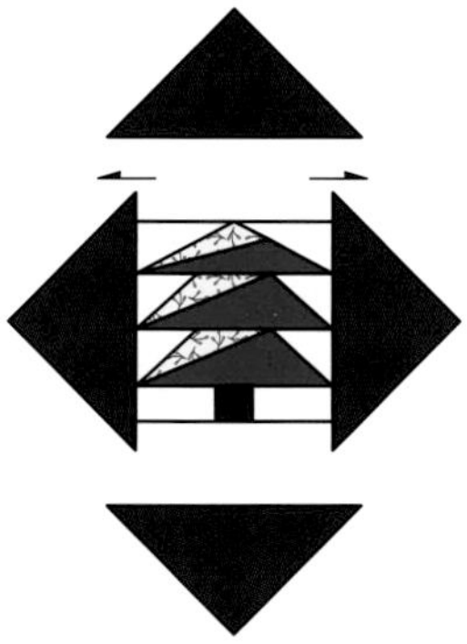

2. Trim the block ¼" from the corners of the Tree block on all 4 sides, squaring the block as you go. Repeat to make the number of Tree blocks required for your project.

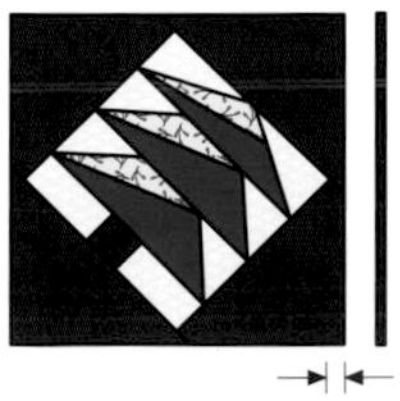

3. Referring to "Adding Setting Triangles" on page 9, sew the dark green print setting triangles between the Tree blocks to form a row. Sew a dark green print end triangle to each end of the row. Trim the top of the Tree row ¼" from the points of the Tree blocks, as shown in the illustration on page 10.

Easy Embellishment

Add some twinkle to your quilt by fusing a star to each setting triangle. Just draw or trace stars onto paper-backed fusible web and follow the manufacturer's directions to fuse yellow-fabric stars to your quilt after assembling the Tree row. Use three strands of embroidery floss to buttonhole stitch around their edges for a folk-art look.

Assembling the Santa Row

1. Sew the 1½" x 3½" dark green print rectangles between the Santa blocks to form a row. Your row should begin and end with a Santa block.

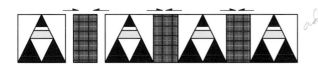

2. Measure and compare the lengths of the Santa row and the Tree row. If the Santa row is shorter, subtract its length from the length of the Tree row, and divide the resulting number in half. Cut 2 additional rectangles, each 3½" long and ½" wider than the number you just calculated. Sew 1 rectangle to each end of the Santa row so it is the same length as the Tree row. Remeasure to make sure your rows are now equal in length.

Assembling the Quilt

Place the Santa row wrong side up and upside down on top of the Tree row. Pin and sew the rows together. Pin the top-of-mantel fabric wrong side up on top of the Santa row and sew the rows together, referring to the assembly diagram below.

Assembly Diagram

Finishing the Quilt

1. Referring to "Layering and Finishing" on page 11, layer the batting, backing, and mantel quilt top, and finish the edges of your quilt.

2. Quilt as desired. The quilt shown was quilted in the ditch along the seams between the top-of-mantel fabric, the Santa row, and the Tree row. You can also stipple quilt the top of the mantel section to make it flatter.

3. With a permanent, fine-tip marker, draw 2 dots for eyes on the face of each Santa, and use a small sponge makeup applicator to add a little blush to the cheeks. Add a tiny pompon with a dot of glue or sew a jingle bell to the top of each Santa hat. Using a double strand of thread, sew a bell or tassel to the bottom point of each Tree block.

Santa Stack Bell Pull

Use the same Santa blocks you made for the mantel quilt to create a 6" x 33" holiday bell pull. It goes together quickly and easily, and the only additional items you'll need are ¼ yard of a Christmas print, a 1" brass ring, eight small jingle bells, and a large tassel.

Begin by making eight Santa blocks, referring to "Paper Piecing" on page 6 and using the cutting chart on page 14 and the Santa block pattern on page 45. Sew the blocks together vertically, removing only the paper in the seam allowances. Cut two rectangles, 2" x 3½" each, from a Christmas print, and sew one to the top and one to the bottom of the stack of Santa blocks. From the same print, cut two strips, 2" x 27½", and sew one to each side of the stack of Santa blocks. Remove the paper from the blocks. Cut a 5¾" x 5¾" square from the same print and cut it diagonally once. Sew the long edges of the resulting triangles to the top and bottom of the bell pull.

Referring to "Layering and Finishing" on page 11, use a 10" x 37" piece of backing and a 10" x 37" piece of batting to layer and finish the edges of the bell pull.

Embellish the Santa faces as for the mantel quilt (see "Finishing the Quilt" on page 15). Hand sew jingle bells to the tops of the Santa hats and the brass ring to the top of the bell pull with a double strand of thread. Hand sew the large tassel to the bottom of the pull. If your tassel is very large, you may want to cover the thick area above the fringe with a scrap of the Christmas print. Just turn under the scrap's raw edges and hand stitch it over the area you want to cover.

Autumn Maples Mantel Quilt

Finished block sizes:
Maple Leaf—6" x 6"; 7¾" across diagonal
Acorn—3" x 3"; 4¼" across diagonal

Materials

Yardages are based on 42"-wide fabric.

- ¾ yd. light print for Maple Leaf and Acorn blocks
- ½ yd. large autumn print for setting and end triangles
- ¼ yd. each of 6 different small autumn prints for Maple Leaf and Acorn blocks
- ⅛ yd. dark miniature check for acorn tops
- ⅛ yd. or scraps of brown for maple-leaf and acorn stems
- Tassels for embellishment

NOTE: Yardages are based on the quilt shown. If your quilt requires more blocks than shown, you may need to buy extra fabric.

Measuring Your Mantel

Refer to "Adapting the Projects" on page 6 to measure the length and width of your mantel. You will need the following additional materials based on these measurements.

Top-of-mantel fabric: 1 piece the size determined
Backing fabric: 1 piece 2" longer and 2" wider than top-of-mantel fabric
Batting: 1 piece the same size as backing fabric

Determining the Number of Blocks

Maple Leaf blocks: Divide the length of your mantel in inches by 7.75. Round down to the next whole number for the number of Maple Leaf blocks to make.
Acorn blocks: Divide the length of your mantel in inches by 4.25. Round down to the next whole number for the number of Acorn blocks to make.

Cutting for One Maple Leaf Block

Cut 1 piece of fabric for each piece number, unless otherwise indicated.

Unit	Piece	Fabric	Dimensions
Top	1	Light print	2¾" x 2¾"
	2, 4	Small autumn print	2¾" x 2¾" ◺ *
	3, 5	Light print	2¾" x 2¾" ◺ *
	6	Small autumn print	2¾" x 6½"
	7	Light print	2¾" x 2¾" ◺ †
Bottom	1, 3	Light print	2½" x 2½" ◺ *
	2	Brown	1¼" x 3½"
	4	Small autumn print	2¾" x 4½"

◺ Cut in half diagonally once to yield 2 triangles.
* *Cut 1 square for these pieces.*
† *Use the extra triangle for piece 5 in the bottom unit.*

Cutting for One Acorn Block

Cut 1 piece of fabric for each piece number, unless otherwise indicated.

Unit	Piece	Fabric	Dimensions
Stem	1	Brown	1" x 2"
	2, 3	Light print	2" x 2" ◺ *
Top	1	Dark miniature check	2" x 3½"
	2, 3	Light print	1" x 1½"
	4, 5	Light print	1¼" x 1½"
	6, 7	Light print	1½" x 2"
Bottom	1	Small autumn print	2¾" x 2¾"
	2	Light print	1" x 1½"
	3	Light print	1" x 2"
	4, 5	Light print	1" x 2½"
	6, 7	Light print	2¼" x 2½"

◺ Cut in half diagonally once to yield 2 triangles.
* *Cut 1 square for these pieces.*

Additional Cutting

From the large autumn print, cut:

1 square, 9½" x 9½", for every 5 Maple Leaf blocks your mantel requires; cut each square diagonally twice to yield 4 setting triangles. (You may have leftover triangles, depending on the number required.)

1 square, 5" x 5"; cut diagonally once to yield 2 end triangles

From among the 6 small autumn prints, cut:

2 squares, 3¼" x 3¼", for each Acorn block; cut each square diagonally once to yield 4 setting triangles

Making the Blocks

Referring to "Paper Piecing" on page 6 and using the cutting charts at left and the patterns on pages 46–47, make the number of Maple Leaf blocks and Acorn blocks your mantel size requires.

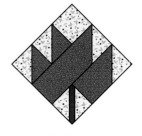

Maple Leaf

Acorn

Assembling the Maple Leaf Row

1. Referring to "Adding Setting Triangles" on page 9, sew the large autumn print setting triangles between the Maple Leaf blocks to form a row. Add a large autumn print end triangle to each end of the row.
2. Trim the top of the Maple Leaf row ¼" from the points of the Maple Leaf blocks, as shown in the illustration on page 10.

Assembling the Acorn Row

1. Sew 2 matching, small autumn print setting triangles to opposite sides of an Acorn block, choosing triangles that contrast well with the fabrics in the block. Press toward the triangles. Sew the 2 matching triangles to the remaining sides. Press toward the triangles.

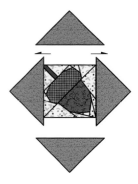

2. Trim the block ¼" from the corners of the Acorn block on all 4 sides, squaring the block as you go. Repeat to make the number of Acorn blocks required for your project.

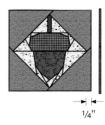

¼"

3. Sew the blocks together to form the Acorn row.
4. Measure and compare the lengths of the Acorn row and the Maple Leaf row. If the Acorn row is shorter, subtract its length from the length of the Maple Leaf row, and divide the resulting number in half. Cut 2 additional rectangles, 4¾" long and ½" wider than the number you just calculated, out of the large autumn print. Sew 1 rectangle to each end of the Acorn row so it is the same length as the Maple Leaf row. Remeasure to make sure your rows are now equal in length.

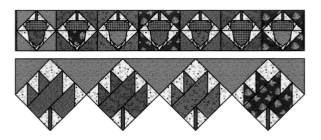

Assembling the Quilt

Place your Acorn row wrong side up and upside down on top of your Maple Leaf row. Pin and sew the rows together. Pin the top-of-mantel fabric wrong side up to the top of the Acorn row and sew the rows together, referring to the assembly diagram below.

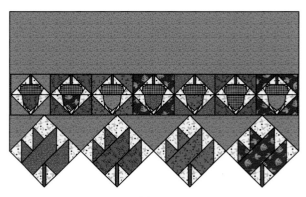

Assembly Diagram

Finishing the Quilt

1. Referring to "Layering and Finishing" on page 11, layer the batting, backing, and mantel quilt top, and finish the edges of your quilt.
2. Quilt as desired. The quilt shown was machine quilted in the ditch along the seams between the top-of-mantel section, the Maple Leaf row, and the Acorn row. It was stipple quilted in the top-of-mantel section and in the large setting triangles.
3. Using a double strand of thread, stitch a tassel to the bottom point of each Maple Leaf block.

Autumn Color Table Runner

Finished size of runner:

48½" x 16½"

Finished block sizes:

Star—8" x 8"
Log Cabin—5⅝" x 5⅝"
Log Cabin Pumpkin—4" x 4"
Maple Leaf—4" x 4"
Acorn—4" x 4"

Materials

Yardages are based on 42"-wide fabric,
unless otherwise noted.

- 1 yd. *total* of 4 small tan prints for background
- 4 fat quarters of small autumn prints, plaids, or checks for the paper-pieced blocks
- 4 fat eighths of different small autumn prints, plaids, or checks for the paper-pieced blocks
- ⅛ yd. or scrap of miniature check for the acorn tops
- ⅔ yd. fabric for backing
- ⅓ yd. fabric for binding
- 21" x 53" piece of batting
- ⅛ yd. paper-backed fusible web
- Black and dark green embroidery floss for buttonhole stitching around pumpkin leaves and for embroidering pumpkin vines

Cutting for One Star Block

Cut 1 piece of fabric for each piece number, unless otherwise indicated.

Unit	Piece	Fabric	Dimensions
A	1	Tan print	4½" x 4½" ⊠*
	2	Autumn print 1	2¾" x 3"
	3	Autumn print 2	4" x 4" ◻†
B	2	Autumn print 1	2¾" x 3"
	4	Tan print	3½" x 3½"
C	2	Autumn print 1	2¾" x 3"
(Cut 2.)			
	3	Autumn print 2	4" x 4" ◻‡
	4, 5	Tan print	3½" x 3½"

◻ Cut in half diagonally once to yield 2 triangles.

⊠ Cut in half diagonally twice to yield 4 triangles.

* *Use the extra triangles for piece 1 in units B and C.*

† *Use the extra triangle for piece 3 in unit B.*

‡ *Cut 1 square; use 1 triangle in each unit C.*

Cutting for One Log Cabin Block

Cut 1 piece of fabric for each piece number.

Piece	Fabric	Dimensions
1	Autumn print	2" x 2"
2	Tan print	2" x 2"
3	Tan print	2" x 2¾"
4	Autumn print	2" x 2¾"
5	Autumn print	2" x 3½"
6	Tan print	2" x 3½"
7	Tan print	2" x 4¼"
8	Autumn print	2" x 4¼"
9	Autumn print	2" x 5"
10	Tan print	2" x 5"
11	Tan print	2" x 6"
12	Autumn print	2" x 6"
13	Autumn print	2" x 6¾"

Cutting for One Log Cabin Pumpkin Block

Cut 1 piece of fabric for each piece number.

Piece	Fabric	Dimensions
1	Autumn print 1	1½" x 1½"
2	Autumn print 2	1½" x 1½"
3	Autumn print 2	1½" x 2"
4	Autumn print 1	1½" x 2"
5	Autumn print 1	1½" x 2¾"
6	Autumn print 2	1½" x 2¾"
7	Autumn print 2	1½" x 3¼"
8	Autumn print 1	1½" x 3¼"
9	Autumn print 1	1½" x 4"
10	Autumn print 2	1½" x 4"
11	Autumn print 2	1½" x 4½"
12	Autumn print 1	1½" x 4½"
13	Autumn print 1	1½" x 5"

Cutting for One Maple Leaf Block

Cut 1 piece of fabric for each piece number, unless otherwise indicated.

Unit	Piece	Fabric	Dimensions
Top	1	Tan print	2¼" x 2¼"
	2, 4	Autumn print	2½" x 2½" ◻*
	3, 5	Tan print	2½" x 2½" ◻*
	6	Autumn print	2¼" x 5"
	7	Tan print	2½" x 2½" ◻†
Bottom	1, 3	Tan print	2¼" x 2¼" ◻*
	2	Autumn print	1¼" x 3"
	4	Autumn print	2½" x 3½"

◻ Cut in half diagonally once to yield 2 triangles.

* *Cut 1 square for these pieces.*

† *Use the extra triangle for piece 5 in the bottom unit.*

Cutting for One Acorn Block

Cut 1 piece of fabric for each piece number.

Unit	Piece	Fabric	Dimensions
Stem	1	Autumn print	1¼" x 2¼"
	2, 3	Tan print	2¼" x 2¼"
Top	1	Miniature check	2¼" x 4¼"
	2, 3, 4, 5	Tan print	1¼" x 2"
	6, 7	Tan print	2" x 2¼"
Bottom	1	Autumn print	3¼" x 3½"
	2	Tan print	1¼" x 1¾"
	3	Tan print	1¼" x 2¼"
	4, 5	Tan print	1¼" x 3"
	6, 7	Tan print	2½" x 3"

Additional Cutting

From the tan prints, cut:

1 square, 10" x 10"; cut diagonally twice to yield 4 setting triangles for the end units

6 squares, 4½" x 4½", cut from different tan prints, for the solid background patches in the pumpkin four-patch units

8 squares, 1½" x 1½", cut from 2 different small tan prints, for the corners of the Log Cabin Pumpkin blocks

From the binding fabric, cut:

4 strips, 2" x 42"

tip If you follow my materials list, you'll have a nice, scrappy quilt, but you could buy greater quantities of fewer fabrics or use scraps of autumn print from your stash to tailor the scrappiness of the quilt to your taste.

Making the Blocks

Referring to "Paper Piecing" on page 6 and using the cutting charts on pages 21–22 and the patterns on pages 48–52, make 4 Star blocks, 2 Log Cabin blocks, 2 Log Cabin Pumpkin blocks, 4 Maple Leaf blocks, and 4 Acorn blocks. Use a variety of the different autumn prints in each block.

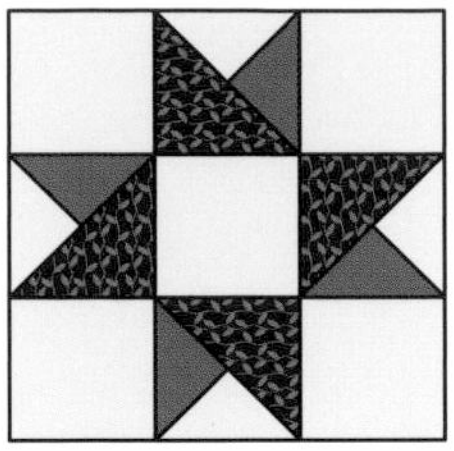

Star
Make 4.

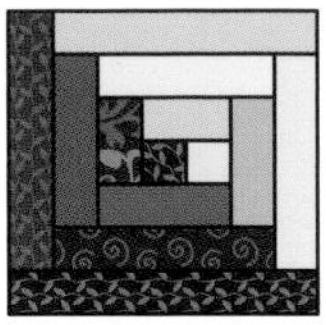

Log Cabin
Make 2.

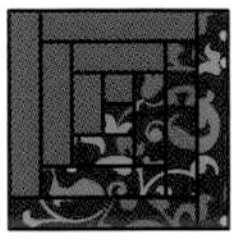

Log Cabin
Pumpkin
Make 2.

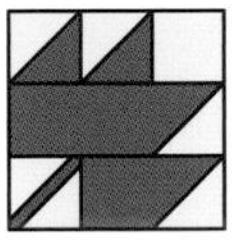

Maple Leaf
Make 4.

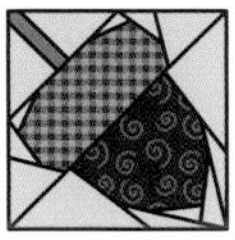

Acorn
Make 4.

Assembling the Log Cabin Block End Units

1. Sew a short edge of a small tan print setting triangle to a tan print side of a Log Cabin block. Repeat on the adjacent tan print side of the block, making sure the excess triangle fabric falls at the top of the unit. Repeat to make a second Log Cabin block end unit.
2. Trim both units ¼" from the corners of the Log Cabin blocks.

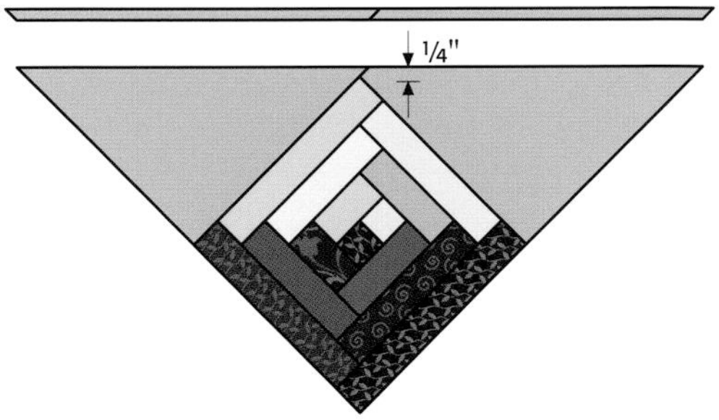

Assembling the Log Cabin Pumpkin Blocks

1. After paper piecing the pumpkins, you'll need to "round off" their corners with the 1½" tan print squares. Place one of the squares right side down in a corner of your block. Making sure that the edges of the square are even with the edges of the block, stitch across each square from corner to

corner. Trim away the excess fabric, leaving a ¼" seam allowance. Repeat for all 4 corners of both Log Cabin Pumpkin blocks, and press toward the squares.

2. Sew each Log Cabin Pumpkin block into a four-patch unit with 3 tan 4½" squares. The row with the Log Cabin Pumpkin block in it will become the "bottom" row of this unit once you fuse the stems and leaves to the runner.

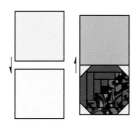 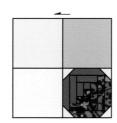

Make 2.

Assembling the Maple Leaf and Acorn Four-Patch Units

Sew 2 Maple Leaf blocks and 2 Acorn blocks into a four-patch unit. Position the Acorn and Maple Leaf blocks as in the photo on page 20, or come up with your own arrangement. Repeat to make a second four-patch unit.

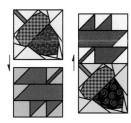 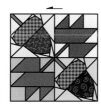

Make 2.

Assembling the Table Runner

1. Referring to the assembly diagram, lay out the Star blocks, Log Cabin Pumpkin four-patch units, and Maple Leaf and Acorn four-patch units. Play with the arrangement of units until it pleases your eye.
2. Sew the blocks together into 2 rows, pressing the seams in opposite directions. Sew the rows together, pressing the center seam open so it lies flat. Attach the Log Cabin block end units to the ends of the table runner.
3. Trace the pumpkin stem and leaf patterns (page 50) onto paper-backed fusible web twice each. Following the manufacturer's directions, cut out the shapes, leaving a generous margin around the outlines. Choose fabrics from among your small autumn prints. Press the stems and leaves onto the wrong sides of the fabrics, and cut them out along the lines.

Assembly Diagram

Fuse 1 stem and 1 leaf to the top of each pumpkin. Use 3 strands of black embroidery floss to buttonhole stitch around the edges of the stems and leaves.
4. Referring to the photo on page 20 and using 3 strands of dark green embroidery floss, backstitch curly vines around the pumpkin stems.

Finishing the Table Runner

1. Layer your table runner, batting, and backing fabric, making sure you have at least 2" of extra batting and backing all the way around.
2. Hand or pin baste the layers together to prevent them from shifting.
3. Quilt as desired. The table runner shown was machine quilted in the ditch between the blocks and in the seams of the setting triangles.
4. Refer to "Layering and Finishing" on page 11 to bind and finish your quilt.

Winter Chill Mantel Quilt

Finished sizes:

Snowman block—8½" x 8½"; 12" across diagonal
Icicle strip—9" x 3"

Materials

Yardages are based on 42"-wide fabric.

- 1 yd. *total* of blue prints for Snowman blocks, setting rectangles and triangles, and icicle strips*
- ½ yd. white print for Snowman blocks and icicle strips
- ⅓ yd. small red check or plaid for setting triangles
- ⅛ yd. or scraps of black solid for Snowman blocks
- Scraps of assorted plaids for Snowman blocks
- Orange carrot buttons or orange embroidery floss for Snowman noses
- Black embroidery floss for Snowman features

* The quilt shown uses 2 different blue prints, but you could use 1 yd. of the same fabric throughout the quilt.

NOTE: Yardages are based on the quilt shown. If your quilt requires more blocks than shown, you may need to buy extra fabric.

Measuring Your Mantel

Refer to "Adapting the Projects" on page 6 to measure the length and width of your mantel. You will need the following additional materials based on these measurements.

Top-of-mantel fabric: 1 piece the size determined

Backing fabric: 1 piece 2" longer and 2" wider than top-of-mantel fabric

Batting: 1 piece the same size as backing fabric

Determining the Number of Blocks

Snowman blocks: Divide the length of your mantel in inches by 12. Round down to the next whole number for the number of Snowman blocks to make.

Icicle strips: Divide the length of your mantel in inches by 9. Round up to the next whole number for the number of icicle strips to make.

Cutting for One Snowman Block

Cut 1 piece of fabric for each piece number.

Unit	Piece	Fabric	Dimensions
Hat	1	Black solid	2" x 3"
	2, 3	Blue print	2" x 2"
	4	Black solid	2" x 5"
Face	1	White print	3" x 5"
	2, 3, 4, 5	Blue print	1½" x 2"
Scarf	1	Blue print	1½" x 2"
	2	White print	2" x 5"
	3	Plaid	2" x 5"
Setting rectangles			
	Top	Blue print	1½" x 4½"
	Left, right	Blue print	1½" x 6½"

Cutting for One Icicle Strip

Cut 1 piece of fabric for each piece number.

Piece	Fabric	Dimensions
1, 13	Blue print	1¾" x 4"
2, 4, 6, 8, 10, 12	White print	2¾" x 4"
3, 5, 7, 9, 11	Blue print	2¾" x 4"

Additional Cutting

From the blue prints, cut:

1 square, 13½" x 13½", for every 5 Snowman blocks your mantel requires; cut each square diagonally twice to yield 4 setting triangles. (You may have leftover triangles, depending on the number required.)

1 square, 7" x 7"; cut diagonally once to yield 2 end triangles

From the small red check or plaid, cut:

2 squares, 5½" x 5½", for each Snowman block your mantel quilt requires; cut each square diagonally once to yield 4 setting triangles for each Snowman block

Making the Blocks

Referring to "Paper Piecing" on page 6 and using the cutting charts at left and the patterns on pages 53–54, make the number of Snowman blocks and icicle strips your mantel size requires.

Snowman   Icicle

Assembling the Snowman Row

1. Sew 2 red check or plaid setting triangles to opposite sides of a Snowman block. Press toward the triangles. Sew 2 more small red check or plaid triangles to the remaining sides. Press toward the triangles again.

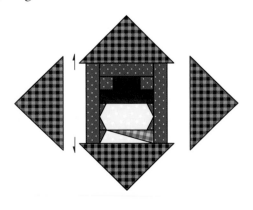

2. Trim the block ¼" from the corners of the Snowman block on all 4 sides, squaring the block as you go. Repeat to make the number of Snowman blocks required for your project.

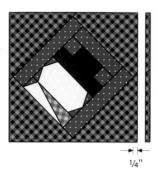

¼"

3. Referring to "Adding Setting Triangles" on page 9, sew the blue print setting triangles between the Snowman blocks to form a row. Add a blue print end triangle to each end of the row. Trim the top of the Snowman row ¼" from the points of the Snowman blocks, as shown in the illustration on page 10.

Assembling the Icicle Row

1. Stitch the icicle strips together along their short edges to form the icicle row.
2. Measure the length of your Snowman row, and trim your icicle row to the same length.

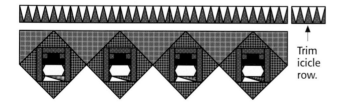

Trim icicle row.

Assembling the Quilt

Place the icicle row wrong side up and upside down on top of the Snowman row. Pin and sew the rows together. Pin the top-of-mantel fabric wrong side up on top of the icicle row and sew the rows together, referring to the assembly diagram below.

Assembly Diagram

Finishing the Quilt

1. Referring to "Layering and Finishing" on page 11, layer the batting, backing, and quilt top, and finish the edges of your quilt.
2. Quilt as desired. The quilt shown was machine stippled in the light areas and outline stitched in the icicle row. Snowflakes were also quilted into the large blue print setting triangles.
3. Use 3 strands of black embroidery floss to give your snowmen French-knot eyes, and make their mouths into half-smiles with outline stitching. I purchased buttons at a craft store to make carrot noses, but the noses could also be stitched with orange embroidery floss. You could also brush a little blush onto each cheek.

Easy Embellishment

For a final wintry touch, use a double strand of thread to attach large sleigh bells to the bottom points of the Snowman blocks.

Winter Chill Wall Quilt

Finished quilt size:
32½" x 43½"

Finished sizes:
Snowman block—4" x 5"
Icicle strip—9" x 3"
Icicle corner—3" x 3"
Tree block—4" x 4"

Materials

Yardages are based on 42"-wide fabric.

- 1¼ yds. blue print for Snowman blocks, icicle strips, and Tree blocks
- 1 yd. white print for Snowman blocks, icicle strips and corners, and Tree blocks
- ¾ yd. black solid for Snowman blocks, inner border, outer sashing strips, and binding
- ⅔ yd. red print for outer border
- ⅓ yd. small red check or plaid for sashing
- ⅛ yd. dark green print for Tree blocks
- Scraps of brown for Tree blocks
- Scraps of plaid for Snowman blocks
- 1½ yds. fabric for backing
- 37" x 48" piece of batting
- Orange carrot buttons or orange embroidery floss for Snowman noses
- Black embroidery floss for Snowman features

Cutting for One Snowman Block

Cut 1 piece of fabric for each piece number.

Unit	Piece	Fabric	Dimensions
Hat	1	Black solid	2" x 3"
	2, 3	Blue print	2" x 2"
	4	Black solid	2" x 5"
Face	1	White print	3" x 5"
	2, 3, 4, 5	Blue print	1½" x 2"
Scarf	1	Blue print	1½" x 2"
	2	White print	2" x 5"
	3	Plaid	2" x 5"

Cutting for One Icicle Strip

Cut 1 piece of fabric for each piece number.

Piece	Fabric	Dimensions
1, 13	Blue print	1¾" x 4"
2, 4, 6, 8, 10, 12	White print	2¾" x 4"
3, 5, 7, 9, 11	Blue print	2¾" x 4"

Cutting for One Icicle Corner

Cut 1 piece of fabric for each piece number.

Piece	Fabric	Dimensions
1	Blue print	3" x 4"
2, 3	White print	2½" x 4¼"
4	White print	2¼" x 3"

Cutting for One Tree Block

Cut 1 piece of fabric for each piece number, unless otherwise indicated.

Piece	Fabric	Dimensions
1	Brown	1½" x 1½"
2, 3 .	Blue print	1½" x 2½"
4, 8	Dark green print	2" x 5"
5, 9	White print	1½" x 4"
6, 7, 10, 11	Blue print	2¼" x 2¼" ◻ *
12	Dark green print	1¾" x 5"
13	White print	1½" x 3¾"
14, 15	Blue print	2¼" x 3"

◻ Cut in half diagonally once to yield 2 triangles.

* *Cut 2 squares for these pieces.*

Additional Cutting

From the black solid, cut:

2 strips, 1⅜" x 42"; subcut each strip into 2 strips, 1⅜" x 14½" and 1⅜" x 25¼"
2 strips, 2¾" x 22¼"
2 strips, 1¾" x 35¾"
4 strips, 2" x 42"

From the small red check or plaid, cut:

3 strips, 2½" x 5½"
4 strips, 2½" x 10½"
2 strips, 2½" x 42"; subcut into 2 strips, 2½" x 23½"

From the red print, cut:

2 strips, 4½" x 16¾"
2 strips, 4½" x 27¾"

Making the Blocks

Referring to "Paper Piecing" on page 6 and using the cutting charts at left and the patterns on pages 45 and 53–54, make 6 Snowman blocks, 10 icicle strips, 4 icicle corners, and 12 Tree blocks.

Snowman Block
Make 6.

Icicle Strip
Make 10.

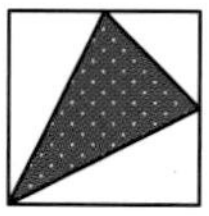

Icicle Corner
Make 4.

Tree Block
Make 12.

Assembling the Quilt

1. Sew the Snowman blocks and 2½" x 5½" red check or plaid sashing strips into 3 rows.

Make 3.

2. Sew the four 2½" x 10½" red check or plaid sashing strips to the tops and bottoms of the Snowman units.

3. Sew one 2½" x 23½" red check or plaid sashing strip to each side of the Snowman units.

4. Sew a 1⅜" x 14½" black solid strip to the top and bottom of the quilt top. Sew a 1⅜" x 25¼" black solid strip to each side of the quilt top.

5. Sew 2 icicle strips together along their short edges. Repeat to make 2 rows. Measure your quilt top horizontally through the center and cut your icicle borders to this length. (These borders should measure 16¼" unfinished.) Sew the borders to the top and bottom of the quilt with the blue triangles pointing toward the quilt, easing as necessary.

6. Sew 3 icicle strips together along their short edges. Repeat to make 2 rows. Measure your quilt top vertically through the center and cut your icicle borders to this length. (These borders should measure 25¼" unfinished.) Add an icicle corner to the top and bottom of each side border. Sew the borders to the sides of the quilt top with the blue triangles pointing toward the quilt, easing as necessary.

7. Sew the two 2¾" x 22¼" black solid strips to the top and bottom of the quilt. Sew the 1¾" x 35¾" black solid strips to the sides of the quilt.

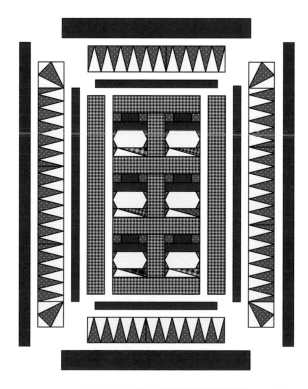

8. Sew the Tree blocks into 4 sets of 2 each.

9. Sew 1 set of Tree blocks to each end of both 4½" x 16¾" red print strips.

Top and Bottom Borders
Make 2.

10. Sew the remaining 4 Tree blocks to each end of the 4½" x 27¾" red print strips to make side outer borders. Attach the side outer borders to the quilt. Attach the top and bottom outer borders from step 9.

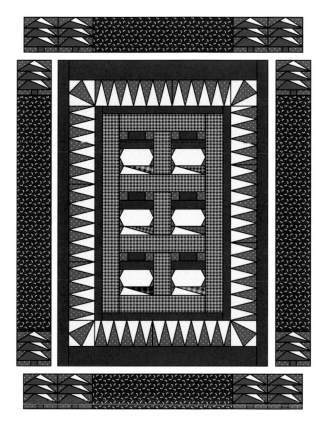

Finishing the Quilt

1. Layer your quilt top, batting, and backing fabric, making sure you have at least 2" of extra batting and backing all the way around. Thread or pin baste the layers together to prevent them from shifting.

2. Quilt as desired. The quilt shown was machine stippled in the light areas and the red borders, and outline stitched around the icicles and Snowman blocks.

3. Refer to "Layering and Finishing" on page 11 to bind your quilt.

4. See step 3 of "Finishing the Quilt" on page 26 to embellish your snowmen.

Waving Flags Mantel Quilt

Finished sizes:

Star block—7" x 7"; 10" across diagonal
Uncle Sam block center—3¼" x 3¼"
Waving Flag block—10" x 3"

Materials

Yardages are based on 42"-wide fabric.

- ¾ yd. red print for Waving Flag blocks and setting triangles
- ⅔ yd. light print for Star blocks, Uncle Sam block centers, and Waving Flag blocks
- ½ yd. navy print for Star blocks
- ¼ yd. starred navy print for Waving Flag blocks
- ⅛ yd. red and light stripe for Uncle Sam block centers
- ⅛ yd. tan solid for Waving Flag blocks
- ⅛ yd. dark burgundy solid for Waving Flag blocks
- ⅛ yd. black solid for Uncle Sam block centers
- Scraps of flesh tone for Uncle Sam block centers
- Scraps of white-on-white for Uncle Sam block centers

NOTE: Yardages are based on the quilt shown. If your quilt requires more blocks than shown, you may need to buy extra fabric.

Measuring Your Mantel

Refer to "Adapting the Projects" on page 6 to measure the length and width of your mantel. You will need the following additional materials based on these measurements.

Top-of-mantel fabric: 1 piece the size determined
Backing fabric: 1 piece 2" longer and 2" wider than top-of-mantel fabric
Batting: 1 piece the same size as backing fabric

Determining the Number of Blocks

Star and Uncle Sam blocks: Divide the length of your mantel in inches by 10. Round down to the next whole number for the number of Star blocks to make. Make 1 Uncle Sam block center for each Star block.
Waving Flag blocks: Divide the length of your mantel in inches by 10. Round down to next whole number for the number of Waving Flag blocks to make.

Cutting for One Star Block

*Cut 1 piece of fabric for each piece number,
unless otherwise indicated.*

Unit	Piece	Fabric	Dimensions
A (Cut 2.)	1	Navy print	3¼" x 3¼"
	2, 3	Light print	2¾" x 2¾" ◺ *
	4, 5	Navy print	3¾" x 3¾" ⊠ †
B (Cut 2.)	1	Navy print	3¼" x 3¼"
	2, 3	Light print	2¾" x 2¾" ◺ *

◺ Cut in half diagonally once to yield 2 triangles.

⊠ Cut in half diagonally twice to yield 4 triangles.

* *Cut 1 square for these pieces.*

† *Cut 1 square for these pieces. Use the extra triangles
for the second unit A.*

Cutting for One Uncle Sam Block Center

Cut 1 piece of fabric for each piece number.

Unit	Piece	Fabric	Dimensions
Hat	1	Black solid	1¾" x 2"
	2, 3	Light print	1¾" x 1¾"
	4	Black solid	1¼" x 3¾"
Face	1	White-on-white	2" x 2½"
	2, 3	Red and light stripe	2" x 2¼"
	4	Flesh tone	1½" x 2½"
	5, 6	Light print	1¾" x 2¾"
Setting rectangles			
	Top, bottom	Light print	¾" x 3¾"
	Left, right	Light print	¾" x 3¼"

Cutting for One Flag Top

Cut 1 piece of fabric for each piece number.

Unit	Piece	Fabric	Dimensions
A	1	Tan solid	1½" x 4½"
	2	Dark burgundy solid	1½" x 1½"
	3	Red print	1½" x 3½"
B	1	Tan solid	1½" x 2½"
	2	Dark burgundy solid	1½" x 1½"
	3	Red print	1½" x 3½"
	4	Light print	1½" x 3"

Additional Cutting

From the light print, cut:

2 strips, 1" x 42", for every 4 Waving Flag blocks
your mantel quilt requires

From the red print, cut:

2 strips, 1" x 42", for every 4 Waving Flag blocks
your mantel quilt requires

1 square, 11½" x 11½", for every 5 Star blocks
your mantel requires; cut each square diagonally
twice to yield 4 setting triangles. (You may have leftover triangles, depending on the number your quilt
requires.)

1 square, 6¼" x 6¼"; cut diagonally once to yield
2 end triangles

From the starred navy print, cut:

1 rectangle, 3½" x 4½", for every Waving Flag
block your mantel quilt requires

Making the Blocks

Referring to "Paper Piecing" on page 6 and using the
cutting charts above and the patterns on pages
55–56, make the number of Star blocks with Uncle
Sam block centers your mantel requires. Use the patterns on page 56 to make a flag top unit A and a flag
top unit B for each Waving Flag block your mantel
requires.

Star Block with Uncle Sam Center

Flag Top Unit A

Flag Top Unit B

Assembling the Star Row

Referring to "Adding Setting Triangles" on page 9, sew the red print setting triangles between the Star blocks to form a row. Sew a red print end triangle to each end of the row. Trim the top of the Star row ¼" from the points of the Star blocks, as shown in the illustration on page 10.

Assembling the Waving Flags Row

1. For every 4 Waving Flag blocks your mantel requires, make 1 strip set using the 1" x 42" red print and light print strips. The strip set will consist of alternating 2 red print and 2 light print strips. Press all seam allowances in the same direction.

2. Subcut the strip sets into 12 sections, each 2½" wide. You'll need 3 sections for every Waving Flag block in your quilt. Flip the center section upside down and sew the 3 strip set sections together to form the bottoms of the Waving Flag blocks.

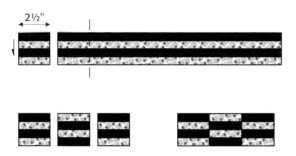

Bottom of Waving Flag

3. Sew the paper-pieced flag top sections together; then sew them to the top of the strip set sections you created in step 2.

4. Sew the 3½" x 4½" starred navy print rectangles to the left end of each flag unit.

Completed Waving Flag Block

5. Sew the Waving Flag blocks together along their short edges to create a Waving Flag row.

Assembling the Quilt

Place the Waving Flag row wrong side up and upside down on top of the Star row. Pin and sew the rows together. Pin the top-of-mantel fabric wrong side up on top of the Waving Flag row and sew the rows together, referring to the assembly diagram below.

Finishing the Quilt

1. Referring to "Layering and Finishing" on page 11, layer the batting, backing, and mantel quilt top, and finish the edges of your quilt.

2. Quilt as desired. The quilt shown was quilted in the ditch along the seams between the top-of-mantel fabric, Waving Flag row, and Star row, and it was stippled in the top-of-mantel fabric and the Star blocks.

3. With a permanent, fine-tip marker, draw 2 dots for eyes on the face of each Uncle Sam, and add a little blush to the cheeks with a small sponge makeup applicator.

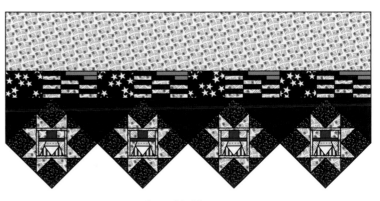

Assembly Diagram

Frankie and Friends Mantel Quilt

Finished block sizes:

Witch, Frankie, Haunted House, and Black Cat—
8½" x 8½"; 12" across diagonal

Bat—8" x 2¼"

Materials

Yardages are based on 42"-wide fabric.

- ½ yd. Halloween print for Witch block and setting triangles
- ½ yd. orange-and-black check or plaid for Bat blocks and triangles around Witch, Frankie, Haunted House, and Black Cat blocks
- ⅓ yd. black solid for Frankie, Black Cat, and Bat blocks
- ¼ yd. black print for Haunted House block
- ¼ yd. Halloween green for Witch, Frankie, Haunted House, and Black Cat blocks
- ¼ yd. dark purple for Witch, Frankie, and Haunted House blocks

- Scraps of gold for Haunted House block
- Scraps of red and dark green for Frankie block
- Red and black embroidery floss for block details

NOTE: Yardages are based on the quilt shown. If your quilt requires more blocks than shown, you may need to buy extra fabric.

Measuring Your Mantel

Refer to "Adapting the Projects" on page 6 to measure the length and width of your mantel. You will need the following additional materials based on these measurements.

Top-of-mantel fabric: 1 piece the size determined

Backing fabric: 1 piece 2" longer and 2" wider than top-of-mantel fabric

Batting: 1 piece the same size as backing fabric

Determining the Number of Blocks

Witch, Frankie, Haunted House, and Black Cat blocks: Divide the length of your mantel in inches by 12. Round down to the nearest whole number for the total number of blocks to make. For a mantel more than 4 blocks long, repeat blocks or use any other 6" Halloween blocks you like.

Bat blocks: Divide the length of your mantel in inches by 9. Round down to the nearest whole number for the number of Bat blocks to make.

Cutting for One Witch Block

Cut 1 piece of fabric for each piece number.

Unit	Piece	Fabric	Dimensions
Top	1	Halloween print	3¼" x 3¾"
	2, 3	Dark purple	3½" x 4"
Bottom	1	Halloween green	4" x 4¼"
	2, 3	Halloween print	3½" x 4¼"
	4, 5	Dark purple	2½" x 4¼"
	6	Halloween print	1½" x 7"

Cutting for One Frankie Block

Cut 1 piece of fabric for each piece number, unless otherwise indicated.

Unit	Piece	Fabric	Dimensions
A	1, 3, 5, 7, 9, 11, 13	Halloween green	1½" x 1½"
	2, 4, 6, 8, 10, 12	Black solid	1½" x 1½"
	14	Halloween green	2" x 5½"
B	1	Dark green	1½" x 4¾"
	2, 3	Halloween green	1½" x 1¼"
C	1	Dark green	1¼" x 1¼"
	2, 3	Halloween green	1¼" x 1½"
	4, 5	Black solid	1¼" x 1¼"
	6, 7	Halloween green	1¼" x 1¾"
D	1	Dark green	1¼" x 2¼"
	2, 3	Halloween green	2¼" x 3"
	4	Halloween green	1½" x 5½"
E	1	Red	1¼" x 3¾"
	2, 3	Halloween green	1½" x 1¾"
	4	Halloween green	2¼" x 5½"
F	1	Dark purple	1¼" x 1½"
(Cut 2.)	2	Black solid	1½" x 1½"
	3	Dark purple	1½" x 6"

Cutting for One Haunted House Block

Cut 1 piece of fabric for each piece number.

Unit	Piece	Fabric	Dimensions
A	1	Black print	1¼" x 1¼"
	2	Orange-and-black check or plaid	1½" x 1½"
	3	Black print	2¼" x 3"
	4	Black print	1" x 4½"
B	1	Black print	3" x 4"
	2	Dark purple	3½" x 3½"
C	1	Halloween green	1½" x 3"
	2	Black print	1¾" x 2¾"
	3	Black print	1¼" x 3"
D	1	Dark purple	1¼" x 1¼"
	2	Gold	1¼" x 1¼"
	3	Halloween green	1" x 1½"
	4	Black print	1½" x 2¾"
E	1	Dark purple	1¼" x 1¼"
	2	Gold	1¼" x 1¼"
	3	Halloween green	1½" x 1¾"
	4	Halloween green	1" x 1½"
	5	Black print	1½" x 3"
F	1	Halloween green	1¾" x 3"
	2	Black print	2¼" x 2¾"
	3	Black print	1½" x 3"
G	1	Dark purple	1½" x 4¼"
	2	Black print	2" x 2½"
	3	Black print	2" x 2¾"
H	1, 3, 5, 7	Gold	1¼" x 1¾"
	2, 4, 6	Black solid	1¼" x 1¾"
	8	Halloween green	1½" x 1¾"
	9, 10	Halloween green	1½" x 2¾"
	11	Black print	2½" x 2¾"
	12	Black print	3" x 3¼"

Cutting for One Black Cat Block

Cut 1 piece of fabric for each piece number.

Unit	Piece	Fabric	Dimensions
A	1, 3	Halloween green	1½" x 1½"
	2, 4	Black solid	1½" x 1½"
	5	Halloween green	2½" x 3½"
	6	Black solid	1½" x 2¾"
B	1	Halloween green	2" x 2¼"
	2	Black solid	2½" x 3¼"
	3	Halloween green	2" x 2½"
	4	Black solid	2¼" x 2½"
	5	Halloween green	1¼" x 2"
C	1	Black solid	1½" x 5¾"
	2	Halloween green	1¼" x 1¼"
	3	Halloween green	1¼" x 2"
D	1	Black solid	2½" x 2½"
	2	Halloween green	2½" x 2¾"
	3	Black solid	3" x 3"
	4	Halloween green	2¼" x 2½"
E	1	Halloween green	2½" x 2¾"
	2	Black solid	1½" x 2¾"
	3	Halloween green	2¾" x 3½"
	4	Black solid	1½" x 2¾"
F	1, 3	Black solid	1½" x 1¾"
	2	Halloween green	1½" x 3¼"
	4	Halloween green	1½" x 2¼"
G	1	Black solid	1½" x 4¾"
	2	Halloween green	1½" x 3¼"
	3	Halloween green	1½" x 7"

Cutting for One Bat Block

Cut 1 piece of fabric for each piece number.

Unit	Piece	Fabric	Dimensions
Top	1	Orange-and-black check or plaid	1½" x 2"
	2, 3	Black solid	1¼" x 1¼"
	4, 5	Orange-and-black check or plaid	2" x 2¼"
	6	Black solid	1½" x 3"
	7, 8	Black solid	3" x 4½"
	9, 10	Orange-and-black check or plaid	2" x 3¼"
Bottom	1	Black solid	2" x 3"
	2, 3	Orange-and-black check or plaid	4" x 4"

Additional Cutting

From the Halloween print, cut:

1 square, 13½" x 13½", for every 5 Halloween blocks your mantel requires; cut each square diagonally twice to yield 4 setting triangles. (You may have leftover triangles, depending on the number required.)

1 square, 7" x 7"; cut diagonally once to yield 2 end triangles

1 strip, 1½" x 42"; subcut into 1½" x 2¾" rectangles to yield 1 fewer rectangle than you have Bat blocks

From the orange-and-black check or plaid, cut:

2 squares, 5¼" x 5¼", for each Halloween block your mantel requires; cut each square diagonally once to yield 4 triangles for each block

Making the Blocks

Referring to "Paper Piecing" on page 6 and using the cutting charts on pages 34–35 and the patterns on pages 57–62, make the number of Witch blocks, Frankie blocks, Haunted House blocks, Black Cat blocks, and Bat blocks your mantel size requires.

Witch

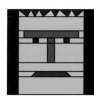
Frankie

Haunted House

Black Cat

Bat

Assembling the Halloween Block Row

1. Sew the long edges of 2 orange-and-black check or plaid triangles to opposite sides of a Halloween block. Press toward the triangles. Sew 2 more orange-and-black triangles to the remaining sides. Press toward the triangles again.

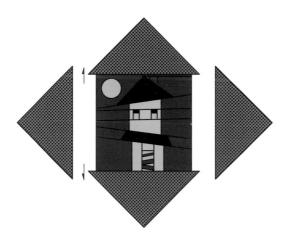

2. Trim the block ¼" from the corners of the Halloween block on all 4 sides, squaring the block as you go. Repeat to make the number of Halloween blocks required for your project.

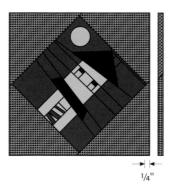

1/4"

3. Referring to "Adding Setting Triangles" on page 9, sew the Halloween print setting triangles between the Halloween blocks to form a row. Sew a Halloween print end triangle to each end of the row. Trim the top of the Halloween block row ¼" from the points of the Halloween blocks, as shown in the illustration on page 10.

4. Trace the appliqué moon found on page 62 onto paper-backed fusible web. Following the manufacturer's directions, fuse the appliqué moon onto the sky in the Haunted House block.

5. Using 3 strands of embroidery floss, backstitch a scar onto Frankie's forehead and/or a trickle of blood at the corner of his mouth. Backstitch a funny nose, 2 French-knot eyes, and a French-knot wart on the witch's face. Give the black cat a red French-knot eye.

Assembling the Bat Row

1. Sew the 1½" x 2¾" Halloween print rectangles between the Bat blocks to make the Bat row.

2. Measure and compare the lengths of the Bat row and the Halloween blocks row. If the Bat row is shorter, subtract its length from the length of the Halloween block row, and divide the resulting number in half. Cut 2 additional rectangles, each 2¾" long and ½" wider than the number you just calculated. Sew 1 rectangle to each end of the Bat block row so it is the same length as the Halloween block row. Remeasure to make sure your rows are now equal in length.

Assembling the Quilt

Place the Bat row wrong side up and upside down on top of the Halloween block row. Pin and sew the rows together. Pin the top-of-mantel fabric wrong side up on top of the Bat row and sew the rows together, referring to the assembly diagram below.

Assembly Diagram

Finishing the Quilt

1. Referring to "Layering and Finishing" on page 11, layer the batting, backing, and mantel quilt top, and finish the edges of your quilt.

2. Quilt as desired. The quilt shown was stipple quilted in the top-of-mantel fabric and in the setting triangles, and the orange-and-black triangles in the Halloween blocks were echo quilted around their outer edges.

Frankie's Spooky Porch Quilt

Give your house a haunted look with this easy 12" x 36" porch quilt. Begin by making and embellishing three Halloween blocks, referring to pages 33–36.

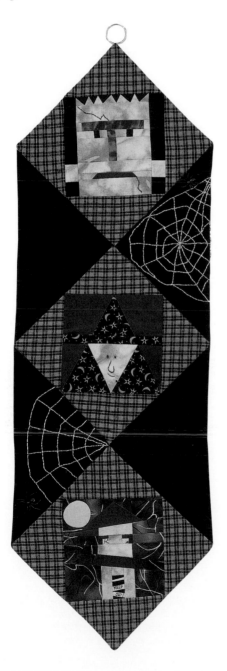

Then, from an orange-and-black plaid, cut six squares, each 5¼" x 5¼". Cut each square diagonally once, yielding twelve triangles, and attach the long sides of two triangles to opposite sides of each Halloween block. Press toward the triangles. Add two more triangles to the remaining sides of the blocks. Press toward the triangles again. Trim the blocks ¼" from the corners of the Halloween blocks (see the illustration on page 36), squaring the blocks as you go.

Cut a 13½" square from black solid fabric. Cut the square diagonally twice, yielding four triangles, and lay out the triangles with your blocks to form three diagonal rows, as shown in the assembly diagram below. Sew the triangles and blocks into rows, then sew the rows together. Trim the triangles ¼" from the corners of the Halloween blocks.

Referring to "Layering and Finishing" on page 11, layer the quilt top on a 16" x 40" piece of backing and a 16" x 40" piece of batting, and finish the edges of your quilt. Quilt as desired, embroidering spiderwebs in the large setting triangles and sewing or gluing spiders to the webs. Hand stitch a brass hanging ring to the top of the quilt.

Assembly Diagram

Baby's Room Window Valance

Finished block sizes:

    Star—5½" x 5½"; 7¾" across diagonal
    Tumbling Block—3" x 3"

Materials

Yardages are based on 42"-wide fabric.

- ½ yd. large bright print for setting triangles and casing
- ⅓ yd. light background print for Star and Tumbling Block blocks
- ⅓ yd. bright blue print for setting triangles
- ¼ yd. *each* of 4 bright prints (pink, blue, yellow, and green) for Star and Tumbling Block blocks
- ⅛ yd. small yellow print for borders above and below Tumbling Block row
- 1 curtain rod the proper length for your valance
- Fray Check

NOTE: Yardages are based on the quilt shown. If your quilt requires more blocks than shown, you may need to buy extra fabric.

Measuring Your Window

Refer to "Adapting the Projects" on page 6 to measure your window and determine the width to make your valance. The length of this valance from casing to block point is 12¼". You will need a piece of backing fabric measuring the width of your valance by the length of the valance (12¼"), plus an extra 2" all the way around.

If you decide to use batting, you'll need a piece of batting the same size as the piece of backing fabric. (See "Batting" on page 5.)

Determining the Number of Blocks

Star blocks: Divide the width of your valance in inches by 7.75. Round down to the next whole number for the number of Star blocks to make.

Tumbling Block blocks: Divide the width of your valance in inches by 3. Round down to the next whole number for the number of Tumbling Block blocks to make.

Cutting for One Star Block

Cut 1 piece of fabric for each piece number.

Unit	Piece	Fabric	Dimensions
A	1	Light background print	2½" x 3"
	2	Bright print	1½" x 2¼"
B	1	Bright print	1½" x 2"
	2	Light background print	2½" x 2¾"
	3	Light background print	2" x 3"
	4	Bright print	2¾" x 5¼"
C	1	Bright print	2¼" x 3"
	2	Light background print	2" x 3"
	3	Light background print	3" x 4¼"

Cutting for One Tumbling Block Block

Cut 1 piece of fabric for each piece number.

Unit	Piece	Fabric	Dimensions
A	1, 4	Light background print	1¾" x 2½"
	2	Bright print 1	2½" x 3¼"
	3	Bright print 3	2¼" x 2½"
B	1, 4	Light background print	1¾" x 2½"
	2	Bright print 2	2½" x 3¼"
	3	Bright print 3	2¼" x 2½"

Additional Cutting

From the large bright print, cut:

One 9½" x 9½" square for every 5 Star blocks your valance requires; cut each square diagonally twice to yield 4 setting triangles. (You may have leftover triangles, depending on the number required.)

1 square, 5¼" x 5¼"; cut diagonally once to yield 2 end triangles

1 strip, 2½" long and as wide as your valance, plus 2" (for the curtain rod casing). This is cut slightly oversize and will be trimmed later. Note: If you are using a curtain rod that has a larger-than-average diameter, you will need to increase the size of the casing strip to be wide enough to fit the rod plus ½" for seam allowances.

From the bright blue print, cut:

2 squares, 4" x 4", for every Star block your valance requires; cut each square diagonally once to yield 4 setting triangles for each Star block

From the small yellow print, cut:

2 strips, 1¼" x 42", for the borders above and below the Tumbling Block row

Making the Blocks

Referring to "Paper Piecing" on page 6 and using the cutting charts at left and patterns on pages 62–63, make the number of Star blocks and Tumbling Block blocks your valance requires.

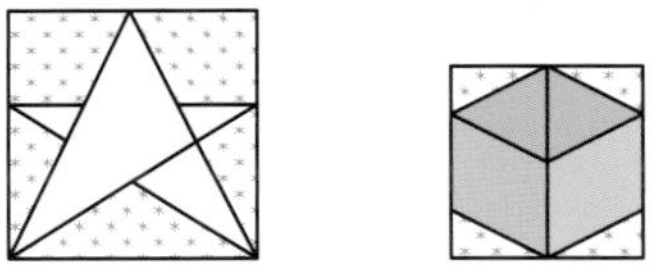

Star   Tumbling Block

Assembling the Star Row

1. Sew the long edges of 2 bright blue triangles to opposite sides of a Star block. Press toward the triangles. Sew 2 more bright blue triangles to the remaining sides. Press toward the triangles again.

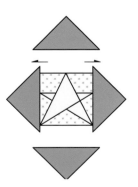

2. Trim the block ¼" from the corners of the Star block on all 4 sides, squaring the block as you go. Repeat to make the number of Star blocks required for your project.

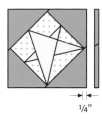

¼"

3. Referring to "Adding Setting Triangles" on page 9, sew the large bright print setting triangles between the Star blocks to form a row. Sew a large bright print end triangle to each end of the row. Trim the top of the Star row ¼" from the points of the Star blocks, as shown in the illustration on page 10.

Assembling the Tumbling Block Row

1. Sew the Tumbling Block blocks together along their short edges to form the Tumbling Block row.

2. Measure and compare the lengths of the Tumbling Block row and the Star row. If the Tumbling Block row is shorter, subtract its length from the length of the Star row, and divide the resulting number in half. Cut 2 rectangles, each 3½" long and ½" wider than the number you just calculated. Sew 1 rectangle to each end of the Tumbling Block row so it is the same length as the Star row. Remeasure to make sure your rows are now equal in length.

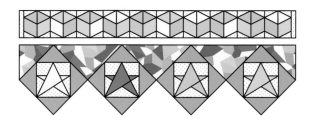

3. Cut the 1¼" small yellow print strips exactly the length of your Tumbling Block and Star rows. Sew 1 strip to the top and 1 to the bottom of your Tumbling Block row.

Assembling the Valance

Place the Tumbling Block row wrong side up and upside down on top of the Star row. Pin and sew the rows together. Pin the casing strip wrong side up on top of the Tumbling Block row and sew the rows together, referring to the assembly diagram below. Trim the casing strip even with the other two rows.

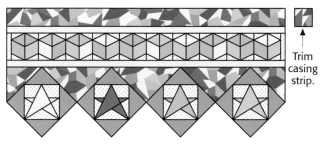

Trim casing strip.

Assembly Diagram

Finishing the Valance

1. Referring to "Layering and Finishing" on page 11, layer the valance top, backing, and batting, if using, and finish the edges of your valance.

2. If you have used batting in your valance, quilt as desired. Stitching in the ditch between the blocks and the setting triangles is usually enough to hold the layers together and give the valance a lightly quilted look.

3. Cut a small slit in the back of each end of the casing large enough for your curtain rod to slip through. Depending on the diameter of your rod, you may want to add a row of stitching to the casing to form a tighter rod pocket. Use a little Fray Check to keep the cut edges from raveling.

Baby's First Little Quilt

Finished quilt size:
  38¾" x 38¾"

Finished block sizes:
  Star—5½" x 5½"; 7¾" across diagonal
  Tumbling Block—3" x 3"
  Corner Star—3" x 3"

Materials

Yardages are based on 42"-wide fabric.

- 1 yd. light background print for setting triangles, Star blocks, and Tumbling Block blocks
- ⅔ yd. *each* of 4 bright prints (pink, blue, yellow, and green) for Star and Tumbling Block blocks
- ⅔ yd. small yellow print for inner and middle borders and binding
- ½ yd. large bright print for outer border
- ½ yd. bright blue print for setting triangles
- 2⅔ yds. fabric for backing
- 48" x 48" piece of batting

Cutting for Star Blocks and Tumbling Block Blocks

The Star block and Tumbling Block block used in this quilt are the same size as the blocks used in "Baby's Room Window Valance." Refer to the cutting charts on page 39.

Cutting for One Corner Star Block

Cut 1 piece of fabric for each piece number.

Unit	Piece	Fabric	Dimensions
A	1	Light background print	2" x 2½"
	2	Bright print	1½" x 2"
B	1	Bright print	1½" x 2"
	2	Light background print	2" x 2½"
	3	Light background print	1¾" x 2¾"
	4	Bright print	2¼" x 4½"
C	1	Bright print	2" x 2½"
	2	Light background print	1¾" x 2½"
	3	Light background print	2¾" x 3½"

Additional Cutting

From the bright blue print, cut:
26 squares, 4" x 4"; cut each square diagonally once to yield 52 setting triangles

From the light background print, cut:
2 squares, 9½" x 9½"; cut each square diagonally twice to yield 8 setting triangles
2 squares, 5¼" x 5¼"; cut each square diagonally once to yield 4 corner triangles

From the large bright print, cut:
4 strips, 3½" x 42"

From the small yellow print, cut:
4 strips, ⅞" x 42"
4 strips, 1½" x 42"
4 strips, 2" x 42"

Making the Blocks

Referring to "Paper Piecing" on page 6 and using the cutting charts at left and on page 39 and the patterns on pages 62–63, make 13 Star blocks, 32 Tumbling Block blocks, and 4 Corner Star blocks.

Star
Make 13.

Tumbling Block
Make 32.

Corner Star
Make 4.

Making the Quilt Center

1. Sew the long edges of 2 bright blue triangles to opposite sides of each Star block. Press toward the triangles. Sew 2 more bright blue triangles to the remaining sides. Press toward the triangles again. (See the illustration on page 39.)

2. Trim the blocks ¼" from the corners of the Star blocks on all 4 sides, squaring the blocks as you go.

3. Sew 9 of the Star blocks into 3 rows of 3 to make the center of the quilt.

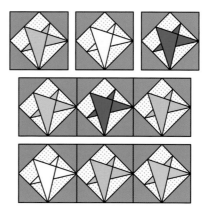

4. Sew the short edges of 2 setting triangles to opposite sides of the remaining 4 Star blocks.

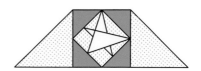

5. Sew a corner triangle to the top of each unit to make 4 corner units.

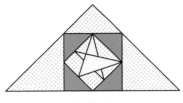

Make 4.

6. Sew 1 corner unit to each side of the quilt top.
7. Trim the quilt ¼" from the points of the blocks on all four sides of the quilt top, squaring the quilt top as you go.

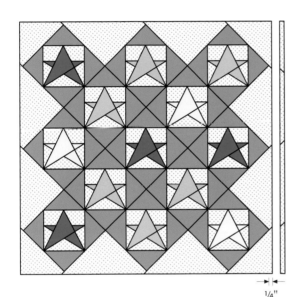

¼"

Adding the Borders

1. Measure the quilt top horizontally through the center and cut 2 of the ⅞" yellow print strips to exactly that measurement. Sew the strips to the top and bottom of the quilt top, easing to fit if necessary. Press seam allowances toward the strips.
2. Measure the quilt top vertically through the center and cut 2 of the ⅞" yellow print strips to exactly that measurement. Sew the strips to the sides of the quilt top, easing to fit if necessary. Press seam allowances toward the strips.

3. Sew 8 Tumbling Block blocks together along their short edges, making sure the blocks are positioned correctly. Repeat to make 4 borders.

Make 4.

4. Sew the pieced borders to the top and bottom of the quilt top. Make sure the rows are positioned so that the tops of the Tumbling Block blocks point away from the center of the quilt.
5. Sew a 3" Corner Star block to each end of the 2 side borders. Remove the paper and sew the side borders to the quilt top. Again, make sure that the Tumbling Block blocks are positioned as shown. Refer to the photo on page 41 for proper Corner Star block placement.

Left Side Border

Right Side Border

6. Measure the quilt top horizontally through the center, including the borders, and cut 2 of the 1½" yellow print strips to exactly that measurement. Sew the borders to the top and bottom of the quilt top, easing if necessary. Press seam allowances toward the 1½" borders.
7. Measure the quilt top vertically through the center and cut the remaining 1½" yellow print strips to exactly that measurement. Sew the strips to the sides of the quilt top, again easing if necessary. Press toward the 1½" borders.
8. Measure the quilt top horizontally through the center and cut 2 of the 3½" large bright print strips to exactly that measurement. Sew the strips to the top and bottom of the quilt top, easing if necessary. Press toward the outer border.

9. Measure the quilt top vertically through the center and cut the remaining 3½" large bright print strips to exactly that measurement. Sew the strips to the sides of the quilt top, easing if necessary. Press toward the outer border.

Finishing the Quilt

1. Cut your backing fabric in half across its width. Cut a 10" strip from the length of one piece, and sew it to the full-width piece. Press the seams open.

2. Layer the quilt top, batting, and backing fabric, making sure you have at least 2" of extra batting and backing all the way around. Thread or pin baste the layers together to prevent them from shifting.

3. Quilt as desired. The quilt shown was quilted in the ditch around the Star blocks and has decorative stitching in the borders.

4. Refer to "Layering and Finishing" on page 11 to bind and finish your quilt.

Assembly Diagram

Patterns

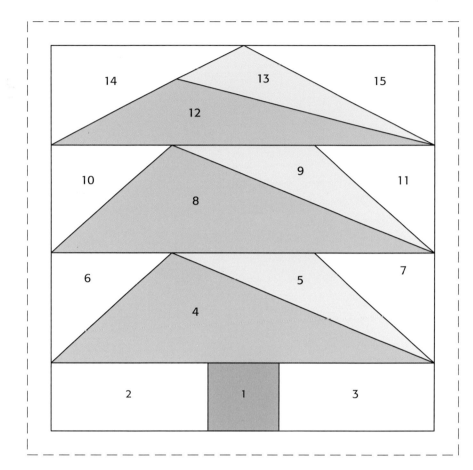

**Christmas Santa Mantel Quilt
Winter Chill Wall Quilt**
Tree

NOTE: To make Tree blocks identical to those in the quilt on page 27, reverse the tree pattern on a photocopier before making your patterns.

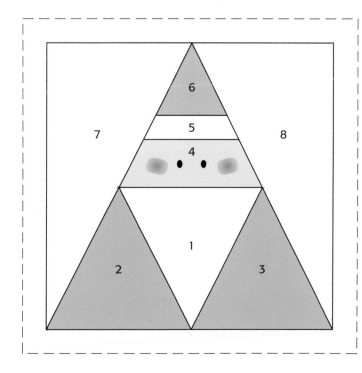

**Christmas Santa Mantel Quilt
Santa Stack Bell Pull**
Santa

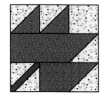

Top

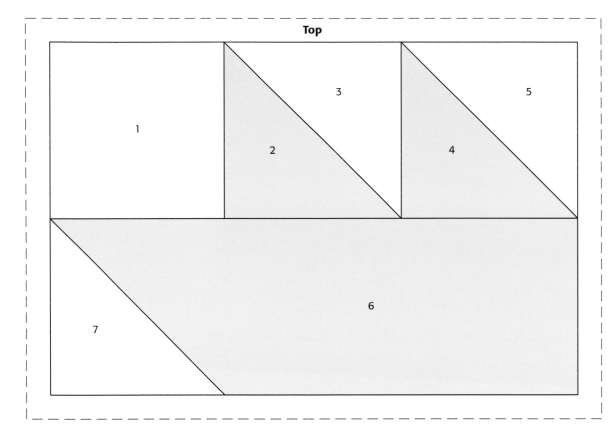

1

2

3

4

5

6

7

Bottom

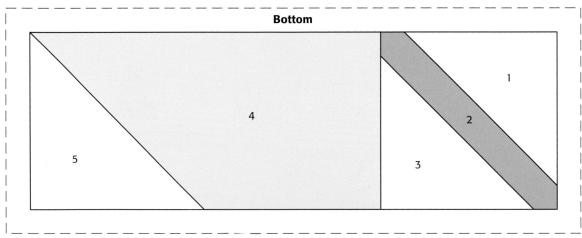

1

2

3

4

5

Autumn Maples Mantel Quilt
Maple Leaf

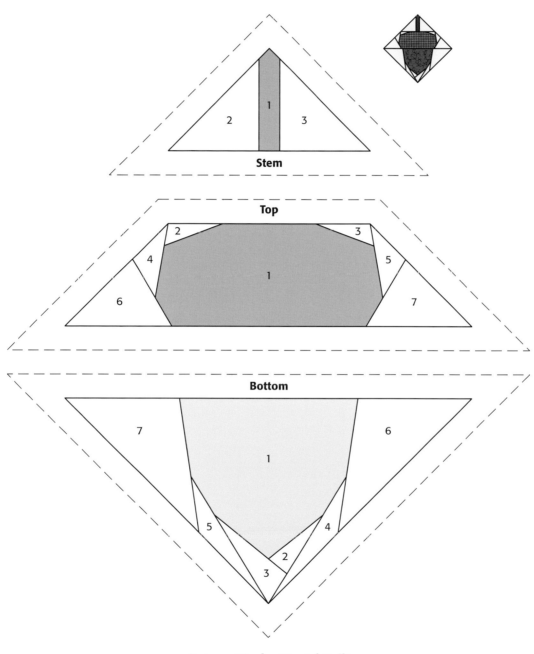

Stem

Top

Bottom

Autumn Maples Mantel Quilt
Acorn

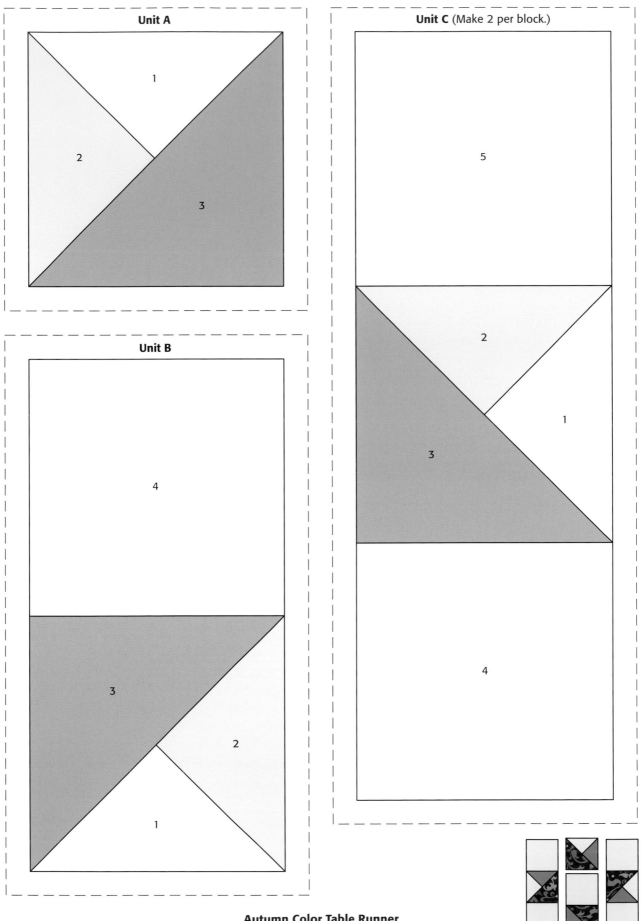

Autumn Color Table Runner
Star

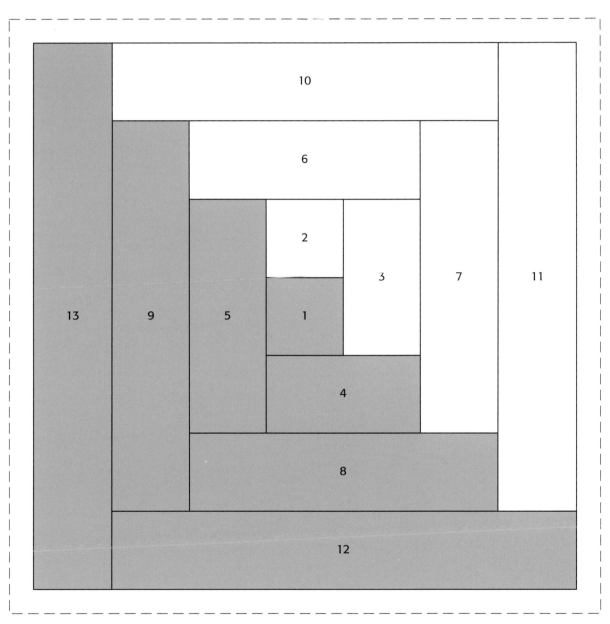

Autumn Color Table Runner
Log Cabin

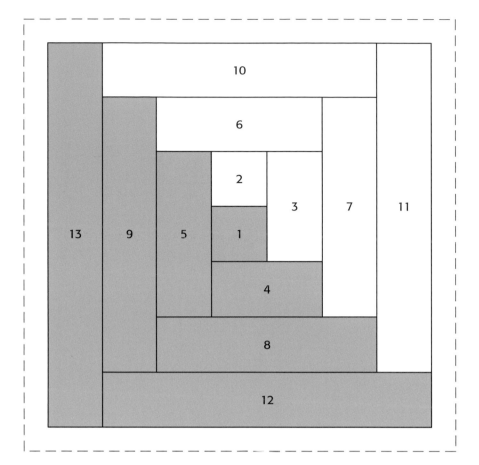

Autumn Color Table Runner
Log Cabin Pumpkin

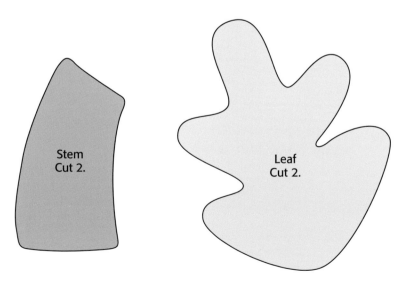

Autumn Color Table Runner
Log Cabin Pumpkin Appliqué Patterns

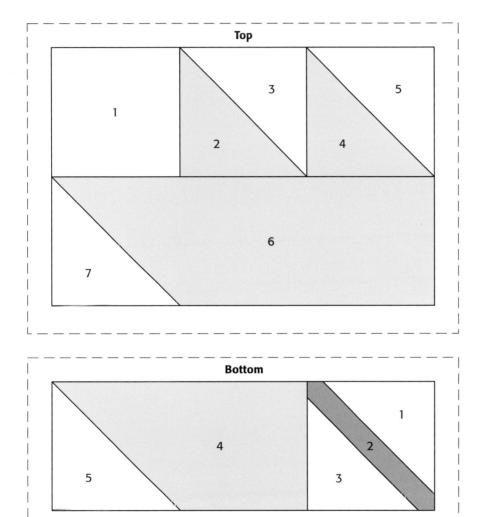

Autumn Color Table Runner
Maple Leaf

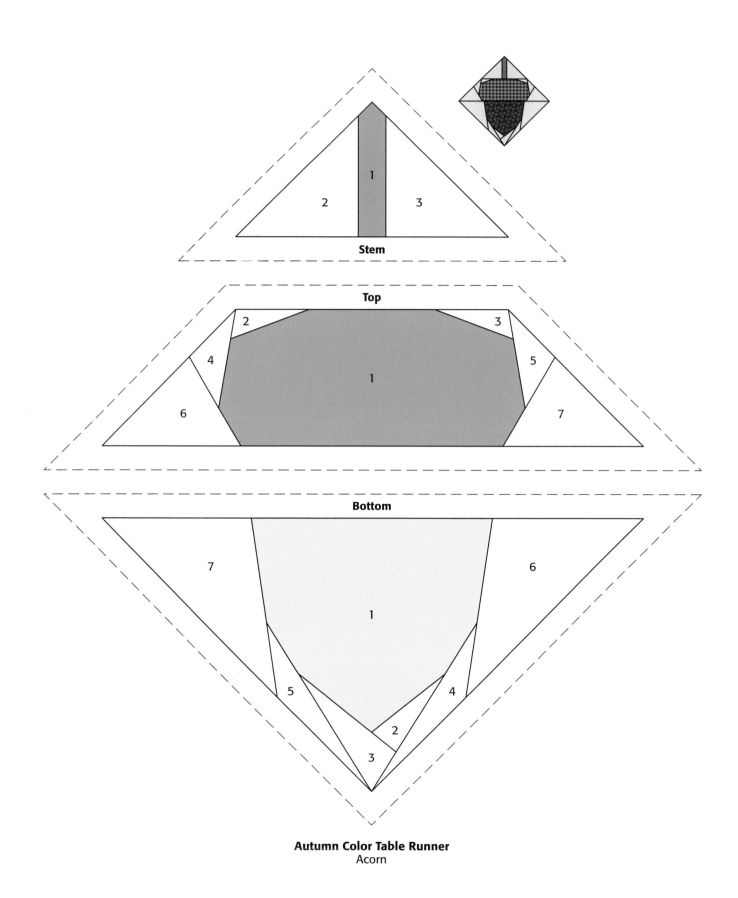

Autumn Color Table Runner
Acorn

1½" x 4½"

1½"
x 6½"

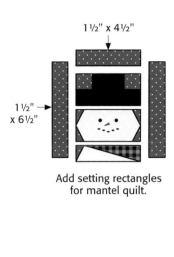

Add setting rectangles
for mantel quilt.

Hat

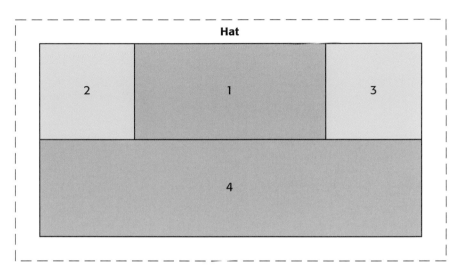

Face

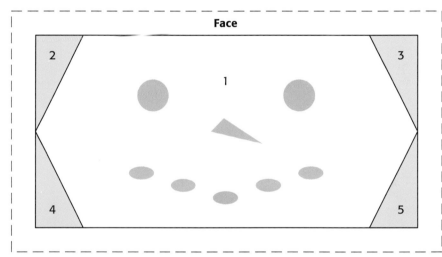

Scarf

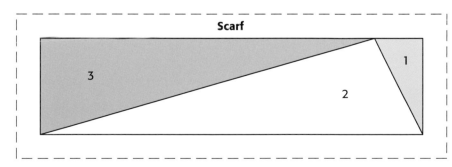

Winter Chill Mantel Quilt
Winter Chill Wall Quilt
Snowman

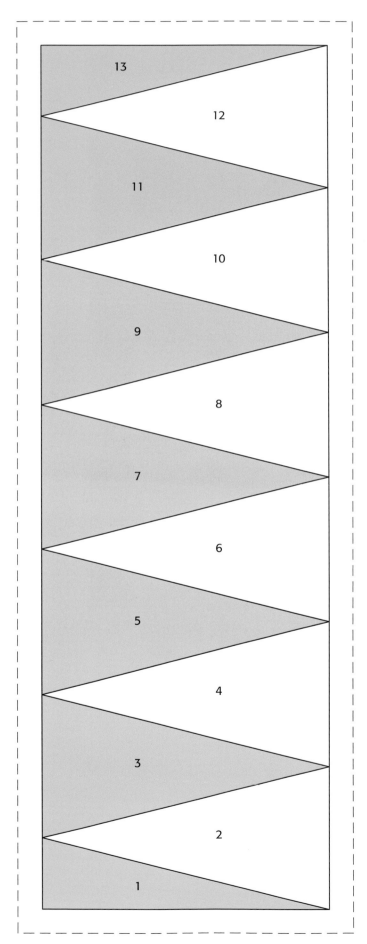

Winter Chill Mantel Quilt
Winter Chill Wall Quilt
Icicle Strip

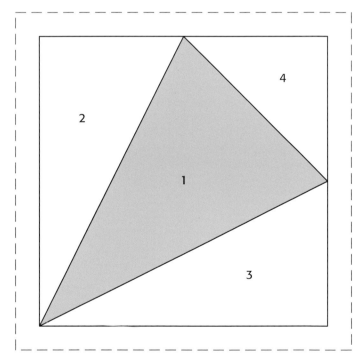

Winter Chill Wall Quilt
Icicle Corner

Unit A (Make 2 per Star block.)

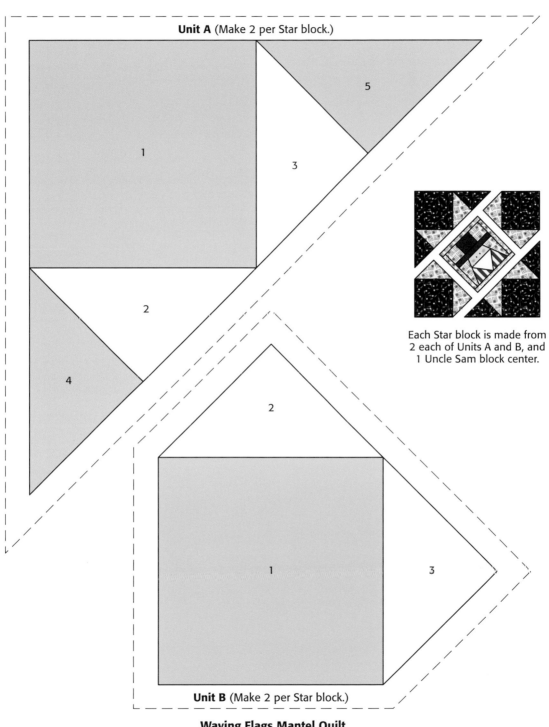

5

1

3

2

4

Each Star block is made from
2 each of Units A and B, and
1 Uncle Sam block center.

2

1

3

Unit B (Make 2 per Star block.)

Waving Flags Mantel Quilt
Star

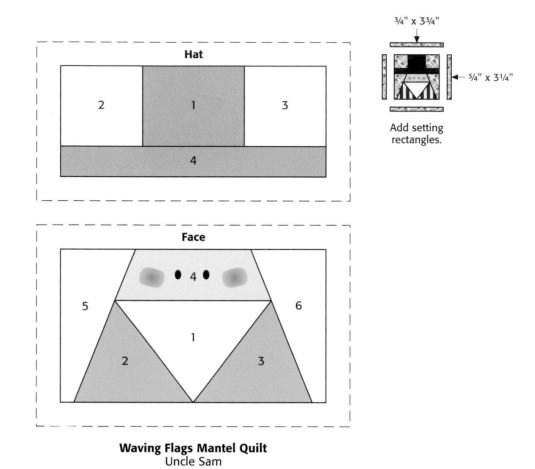

Waving Flags Mantel Quilt
Uncle Sam

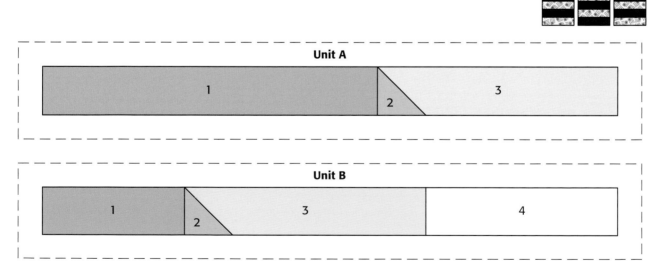

Waving Flags Mantel Quilt
Flag Top

Top

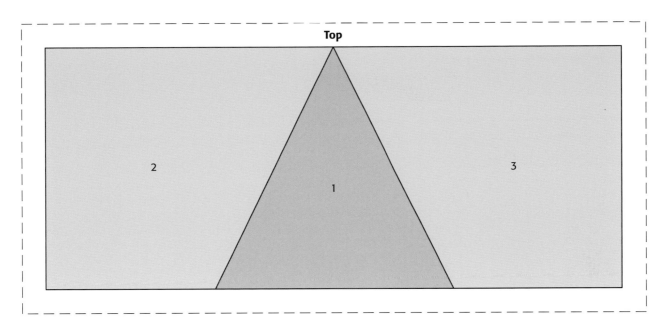

Bottom

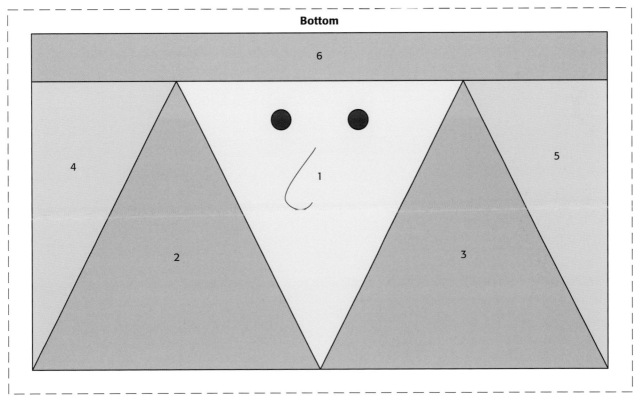

Frankie and Friends Mantel Quilt
Witch

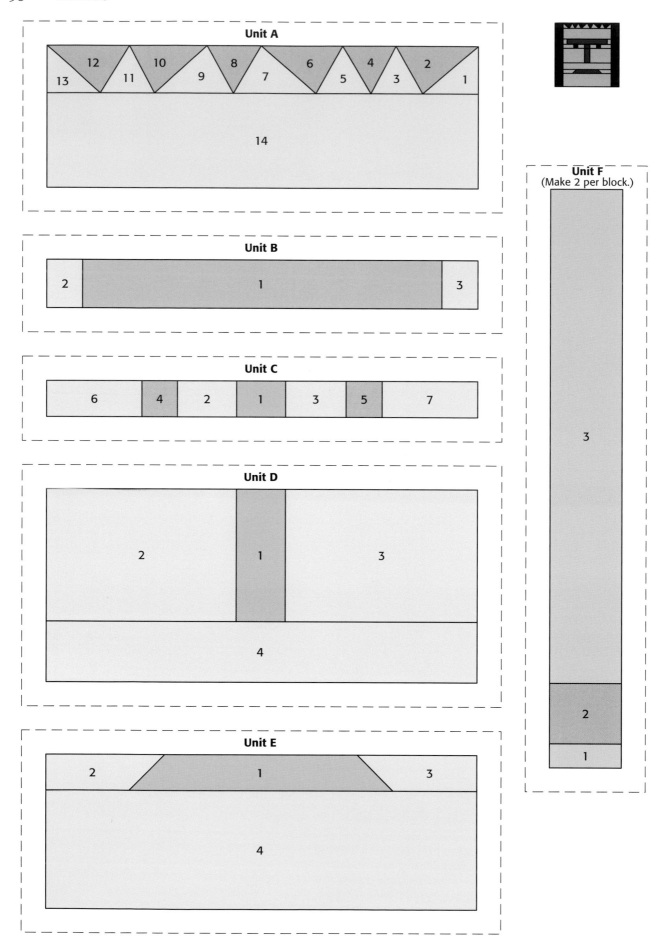

Frankie and Friends Mantel Quilt
Frankie

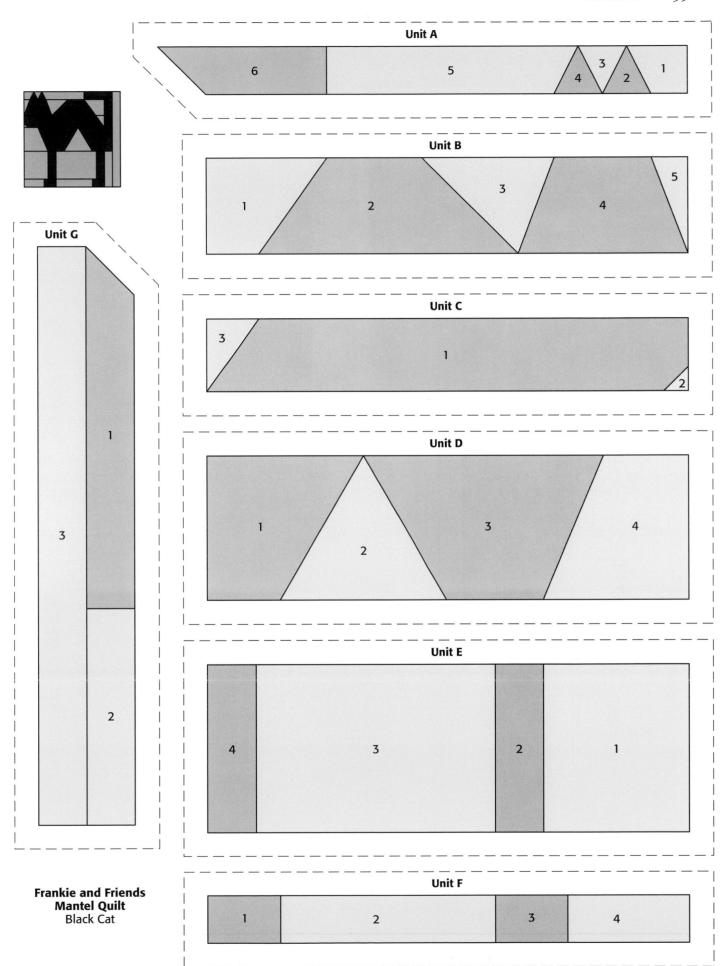

**Frankie and Friends
Mantel Quilt**
Black Cat

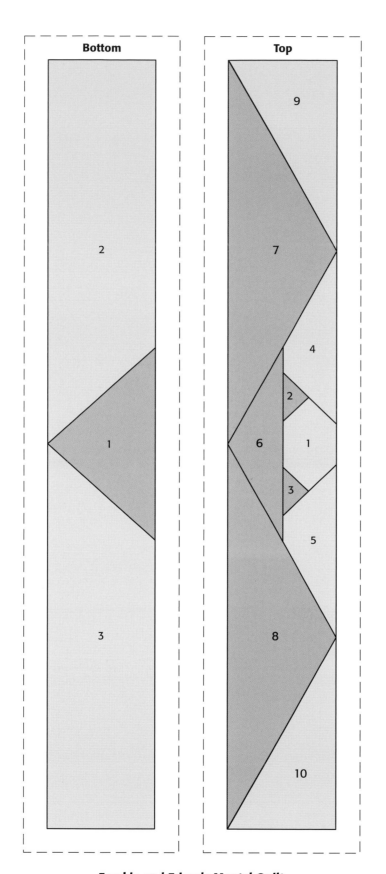

Bottom

Top

Frankie and Friends Mantel Quilt
Bat

Unit H is on page 62.

Unit A

4

2 1

3

Unit B

2

1

Unit C

2

1

3

Unit D

4

3 1

2

Unit E

3 1

2 4

5

Unit F

2

1

3

Unit G

2

1

3

Frankie and Friends Mantel Quilt
Haunted House

Frankie and Friends Mantel Quilt Appliqué Moon

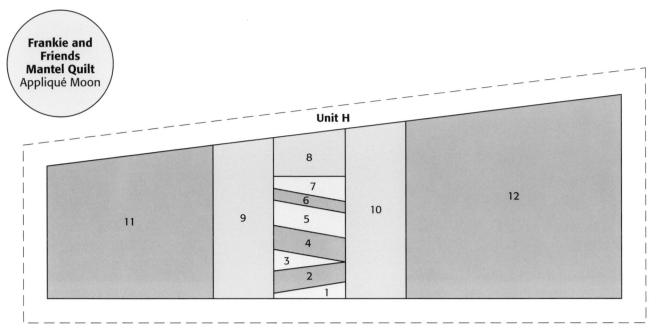

Unit H

Frankie and Friends Mantel Quilt
Haunted House

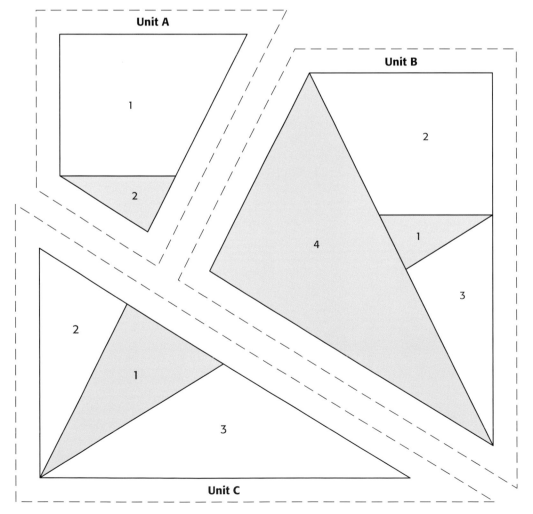

Unit A

Unit B

Unit C

Baby's Room Window Valance
Baby's First Little Quilt
Star

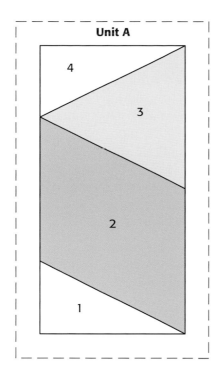
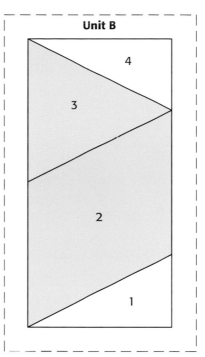

Baby's Room Window Valance
Baby's First Little Quilt
Tumbling Block

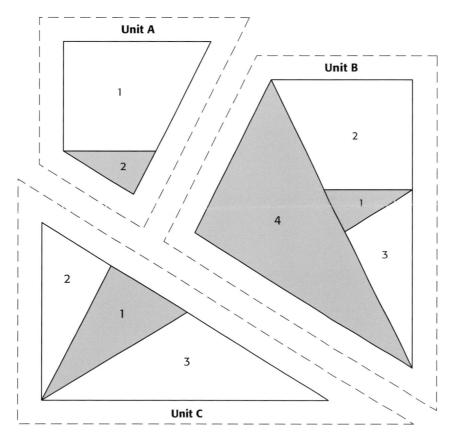

Baby's First Little Quilt
Corner Star

About the Author

Susan Thomson is an award-winning quilter who has been quilting for twenty-three years and teaching quilting in the Houston area for more than thirteen years. She co-founded the Quilt Guild of Greater Victoria (Texas) with wearable artist Judy Murrah in 1983, and she founded the West Houston Quilters Guild in 1993; she currently serves on their board of directors. In 1998, she and her husband, John, started their pattern company, Stitches from Home. Their line of patterns features designs for every room in the house, including the popular Mantel Quilt line. With the help of distributors, the patterns are sold in quilt shops throughout the country. The business is a joint effort, with Susan handling the creative process and stitching and John taking care of the computer design and business aspects. All of the patterns are paper pieced—a technique Susan fell in love with for its speed and accuracy—and they are all taught at Quilt 'n Sew Studio in Katy, Texas, where Susan has been teaching since it opened in 1994.

Susan and John have three children: Travis, twenty-three; Matt, twenty-one; and Amy, nineteen. Susan and John live in Houston, Texas, with their dog, Josie, and cat, Speedy. When not designing or quilting, Susan enjoys gardening, cooking, and baseball.